P9-AQG-994

Familiar Strangers

Doubleday

New York

London

Toronto

Sydney

Auckland

Familiar
Strangers

uncommon wisdom
in unlikely
places

Gotham Chopra

This book is dedicated to all the strangers everywhere
in times of both war and peace
who make life worth living.

PUBLISHED BY DOUBLEDAY
a division of Random House, Inc.
1540 Broadway, New York, New York 10036

DOUBLEDAY and the portrayal of an anchor with a dolphin are trademarks
of Doubleday, a division of Random House, Inc.

Book design by Ellen Cipriano

Library of Congress Cataloging-in-Publication Data

Chopra, Gotham, 1975–
Familiar strangers : uncommon wisdom in unlikely places / Gotham
Chopra.—1st ed.
p. cm.
1. Meditations. I. Title.

BL624.2 .C487 2002
158'.128—dc21
2001047837

ISBN 0-385-49967-1

Copyright © 2002 by Gotham Chopra

All Rights Reserved

PRINTED IN THE UNITED STATES OF AMERICA

May 2002

First Edition
1   3   5   7   9   10   8   6   4   2

Contents

A Note from the Author

The story of Siddhartha Buddha is fairly simple. It's about a boy born into privilege who, despite having every luxury afforded to him, being adored by his family, and worshiped by his people, discovers that one thing eludes him—peace of mind.

Despite having his life already mapped out, for he is destined to inherit an entire kingdom, early one morning the crowned prince Siddhartha sheds his royal robes in exchange for the plain orange ones worn by mendicants who wander the countryside in search of enlightenment. This also becomes the young man's pursuit—enlightenment—freedom from the material and spiritual constraints that bind everyone.

Like all good stories, Buddha's is littered with details that make it both dramatic and touching. But, in essence, its real drama is in chronicling one man's journey from prince to pauper to real power. In my own reading of Buddha's life story, I have pulled nine steps from his life—from his fated birth to his eventual death—and traced them as I've seen them throughout the modern world. Stories like Buddha's that are mythological in their scope have themes and story arcs that are timeless. But their real meanings are resonant only when we are able to see if and how they play out in the real world.

So here are nine steps drawn from the life story of Siddhartha Buddha—fate, fear, refuge, surrender, discipline, temptation, freedom, compassion, and finally death—which I have tried to look at through today's world, through my own experience. I like to think of them as steps along our collective path. Not all of them are clear footprints. They are merely representative of the world that they come from—full of pilgrims on a journey toward a deliverance we all yearn for—the answers to why we are here in the first place and what our individual and collective purposes are are not always provided. Nonetheless, I hope you enjoy reading this book as much as I enjoyed living it. Happy reading.

—*Gotham Chopra*

Foreword

By the summer of 2001, after several years out on the road re-
covering stories for this text, I had triumphantly put pen to
paper for the last time for this endeavor. Then one September
morning the world changed.

On Tuesday, September 11, 2001, at 8 A.M. I boarded a
flight in New York headed for Los Angeles. Shortly we rolled
out onto the runway, lurched back, fired down the long stretch
of pavement, and soared into the sky. It must have been almost
8:30 A.M. when I looked over my shoulder and gazed out at the
New York skyline noting the clear view from Columbia University, my alma mater, all the way down to the World Trade
Center. *What a beautiful day,* I thought to myself. *I wish I wasn't
leaving.* I then closed my eyes and drifted off to sleep.

A little over ninety minutes later I awoke when the pilot's
voice came over the loudspeaker. "Ladies and gentlemen," he
announced in a calm voice, "we are making an emergency landing in Cincinnati because of an apparent terrorist attack in the
New York area. Please stay calm . . ."

There was a nervous murmur throughout the cabin. The

journalist in me demanded immediate information and I reached for the phone. I quickly ran my credit card through the phone, waited for the dial tone, and dialed our News Desk in Los Angeles. The phone cackled, but when the other line picked up, there was no mistaking the panicked tone in one of my colleagues.

"Are you okay?" she asked.

I am. I asked for further information.

"Two planes crashed into the World Trade Center. They're coming down. Oh, My God, they're coming down . . ."

The phone cut off and went dead. I frantically redialed.

No luck.

I tried my sister in Los Angeles.

No luck.

I slowly sat back in my chair and began to panic. I knew my father had flown out of New York on a different flight about an hour before me. I knew my mother was on a flight originating in London destined for San Diego. My fiancée—a fourth-year medical student—worked in New York City. I tried to meditate and tell myself that everyone would be okay. Tears burned my eyes.

When we touched down twenty minutes later, the pilot instructed us not to turn on our cell phones. He gave us instructions to immediately evacuate the plane and follow the instructions of security personnel. We did.

Finally in the terminal, I reached for my phone and turned it on. There I stood huddled with hundreds of other interrupted passengers and gazed up at the television. The fresh images of two smoldering stumps—the remains of the towers of the World Trade Center—played on the screen. Finally I got in touch with my sister, Mallika, who was sobbing on the other end of the phone.

I'm okay . . . where's Papa . . . where's Mom?

Mallika supplied all of the answers—everyone was safe. She had managed to speak to my fiancée as well, who was already at one of the local hospitals doing whatever she could to help. I placed my next call again to the office. I knew that there was work at hand. Sure enough, I already had a car reserved and was destined back for New York. At the rental agency, there was a great shortage of cars. People in line started shouting out their destinations and everyone began carpooling. I joined two other men from the New York area and we were off. Over the next twelve hours we listened closely to the radio as details of the terrorist attack emerged. Every five minutes the name of another family member or friend popped into my head and I dialed the number frantically. Most New York numbers were jammed or out of service. One friend I was able to contact informed me that he was unable to contact someone we both knew. He worked in the 105th floor of one of the towers. He was scheduled to attend an 8:30 meeting. Someone from the meeting had called to say they had survived the initial attack and were waiting for a rescue team. No one had heard from any of them since.

As we cut through the rural countryside of Ohio and then Pennsylvania, I chatted intermittently with the two strangers I had teamed up with.

"Does this mean we go to war?" one of them said softly.

There was a silence in the car.

"This means we've already been at war," the other gentleman said warily. "This sort of violence perpetuates external war, but it is the product of an internal one."

In about half an hour, we stopped at a lonely gas station by the side of the highway. By the driveway a decrepit horse-drawn cart lay on the grass, young Amish gentlemen reclined in the shaded seating area listening to an old transistor radio.

"Good afternoon, sir," he greeted me as I walked toward a pay phone near the cart. "Phone doesn't work, I am afraid."

"It's nice here," I remarked to him, taking in the glorious sunset that was at hand.

"Yes, it is." He lowered the volume on his radio. "Try to take a bit of this with you wherever you are going."

I nodded.

"Tell whomever you meet wherever you are going that a stranger sends his love and his prayers."

We exchanged another nod of acknowledgment and I climbed back into the car.

Finally, just after midnight, we made it just to the edge of New York City, in Fort Lee, New Jersey. There would be no crossing into Manhattan Island—all the bridges and tunnels had been sealed. I spent the night in New Jersey unable to sleep much. At about 2 A.M., for the first time, I made contact with my fiancée who was safe and sound at home. We both cried softly into the phone. By 6 A.M., I was dressed and ready to get in to the city. The only way to get across the river was via the commuter trains, which were offering limited services. As we pulled toward the station in Hoboken, New Jersey, the trains slowed to a stop. There on the other side of the river they stood, like ashen smoking gravestones, the ruins of the twin towers. The train car was silent as everyone gazed out the window. A young woman beside me began to whimper. Another man lowered his head into his hands and muffled his sobs.

Back in the city, people walked around in a daze. The streets were empty of cars but full of wandering pedestrians, walking directly down the middle of Broadway and Fifth Avenue. As we made our way downtown (I had already hooked up with a TV crew), we noticed small cafés open and people filling the outside sidewalk seats. People sat mostly in silence gazing upwards at the thick plume of white smoke still snaking its way westward. At West Fourth Street, a group of kids played basketball. At one point the ball rolled out of play. A young shirtless boy ran after the ball and bent down to pick it up. When he lifted his head, he looked up at the air at the same thick trail of smoke. He shook his head and wiped away something from his eyes—either sweat or tears—and turned away.

Walking home, I stopped and talked to a police officer. After chatting a few minutes, the officer asked me if I would like to see ground zero. I agreed to stay just at the edge away from the workers. The pictures on television of the devastation caused by Tuesday's attack did the scene of the crime absolutely no justice. In real life it appeared as if an asteroid had hit the lower part of Manhattan. Charred, twisted slabs of metal and concrete curled in every direction. It was unfathomable, unspeakable, incomprehensible.

On Wednesday night, while in a cab returning from work to my apartment, I noticed the Muslim name of my driver. He noticed the tone of my skin in the rearview mirror. He nodded at me. On the radio, the commentator was relaying a warning to all men of Middle Eastern and South Asian descent—to be wary of unwarranted violent reprisals from agitated residents of the city.

The taxi driver again looked at me through the mirror and smiled ironically, "We love America. It is our home." He shook his head. "But I think we're fucked."

About a month before that fateful day, I rode up with two colleagues to the Northwest Frontier region of Pakistan bordering Afghanistan. We were covering a story on Islamic militancy training grounds based in Pakistani religious schools. In the

West they had widely been reported to be ground zero for the grooming of young Muslim boys into hostile anti-Western terrorists. In Pakistan, both the government and the men at the school hotly contested these claims, castigating the West for generating such racist propaganda. I traveled to this lost area with as little bias as possible—but with a certain and undeniable fear in my heart.

In the school itself, the chancellor—or head Mullah as he was called—was most kind and hospitable. He had us tour the grounds of the school, meet teachers and some of the boys—though at first we weren't allowed to talk to them. We were then escorted into his private residence. The first thing I noticed on the center table was a bowl of big yellow mangoes and a picture. The picture was of our host—an older Muslim Mullah wearing a traditional white turban and a stained orange beard and his friend—Osama bin Laden, the number-one man on the FBI's list of Most Wanted. I asked our host if we could interview him. He agreed but insisted first that we share mangoes with him. I agreed and he took out a long knife and proceeded to slice the fruit for me. We slurped and chatted for a while.

"Don't get mangoes like this in Los Angeles, do you?"

I shook my head and wiped the juice from my chin.

Finally we were permitted to turn on the camera. I asked the Mullah a wide array of questions. *Did he hate the United States? Why is there such anti-Americanism in this part of the world? Should Americans be afraid?*

He answered them all eloquently and without hostility. He talked about the history of the United States and Afghanistan, how during the Cold War, they were allies, united fighting a war against the Soviets.

"You gave us weapons and trained our men. You built our roads, fed our people. You made us your friend."

"But then your Cold War ended," he said with the only hint of animosity we would see that day, "and because it was no longer in your selfish interest to have us as your allies, you abandoned us, left our people, hungry, and hateful. You turned your friends into foes because you used us like whores."

There was a silence between us.

Finally I asked him about the picture, about the nature of his relationship with Mr. bin Laden.

"He's an old friend. And a good man."

I shook my head. *Is he a terrorist?*

"We don't call him that here." The Mullah made it clear he was not interested in talking anymore. We shook hands. I thanked him for his hospitality.

On the way out, I thought about that hospitality. I knew that the Mullah himself had endorsed a *fatwa,* or religious order, by bin Laden several years ago urging Muslims to kill American civilians. But here was this man cutting mangoes for us and being very gracious.

"Isn't it ironic," he smiled at me, "today a friend and to-morrow, perhaps a foe?" It was not the first time, amazingly enough, I had heard this expression.

"I hope that I never see you as my enemy," the Mullah said to me calmly, "because then, yes, it would be my duty to kill you. It is not between you and me, I think. It is the world around us."

I am not sure how this life lesson resolves. I hope it is not true that the world exerts more influence on us than our intimate interactions with one another. The past few years and months have involved me in many curious encounters—the most recent of which involve an old Mullah in rural Pakistan and a young Amish in rural Pennsylvania.

Back in New York, the day of the terrorist attack, our President proclaims war and tells all of us to prepare like warriors readying for battle. I am not sure whom we will be fighting. I want to go to my favorite café in the city—a small Egyptian place on the Lower East Side that I had been going to since college. The waiters—mostly young Middle Eastern guys who like to talk about basketball and soccer, who come and sit at your table and share a puff on the sweet tobacco hookas they serve there—they are my friends. But I'm not sure when it will open again, if it will open again. There is a mosque next door that has been closed since the attack.

The weeks and months and perhaps even years ahead promise to be complex and wary. Hopefully our leaders will be judicious, precise, and compassionate in the difficult decisions that lay ahead. But it is each of us, it is the codes among us, the ways in which we choose to treat one another and acknowledge our shared humanity that will most carve out our future together on this planet. It is the encounters, the conversations, the whispers between friends and strangers that will most define the world that we live in. While we all must now honor those who lost their lives on September 11, 2001, we must also move forward. Each of us has our story where we were the day the Twin Towers toppled—dramatic and tragic. We also have a lifetime of stories—poignant and pointless—each one of which holds some secret for moving forward. Here are some of mine.

Preface

Backward Bibles,
Blue Trucks, and Hookers

In the city of Guangzhou, China, there's a park where an old man for a couple of hours a day walks backward. He walks in a straight line about one hundred yards back and forth with a permanent toothless grin. It's a nice setting, this park, an oasis of greenery amid the sprawling concrete of one of China's most prosperous provinces. During these autumn days, rows of bright red flowers line the foreground. Behind the man, casting a long afternoon shadow over his path, is a monument of the martyrs—the original socialist "freedom fighters" who staged a revolt in 1911 that was eventually completed in 1949, when the People's Republic of China was officially installed with its Communist regime. The monument is a stiff, brawny arm. It starts at about the elbow and reaches skyward with a rifle clenched in its hand, raised in either defiance or triumph. The old man continues his backward walking, back and forth, back and forth, pausing for a moment to stare up at the statue. He does this regularly, pausing midway in his journey to look up at it as if he's never seen it before. When I have a chance to talk with him, he tells me how much he enjoys what he does. He says he's been doing the walk for twenty years, every single day without fail.

It's hard to know if the old man is telling the truth, because if you weren't here yesterday, the day before, have no plans to be here tomorrow or the day after and so on, then you'll never know. I'm not sure what I think of him, but there is something about him, his walk, maybe his smile, that I know I quite like.

A middle-aged Chinese woman who moments ago was skillfully slicing a pear for me has just shoved me into the corner. She then pulls the shades shut, dims the lights, closes the cupboard, and shoots to the doorway. As she opens it, she turns toward me, lifts a finger to her pursed lips—whispers, "Shhh"—and pulls the door shut, locking it from the other side. This leaves me all alone, sitting in the dark.

The room I am locked in sits in the middle of a large, decrepit, abandoned compound in a derelict town in central China. At one time this mining town's biggest factory employed nearly ten thousand workers. Today, as a result of the Chinese government's widespread privatization of formerly state-owned factories, that number is closer to one thousand. The town itself is a virtual wasteland. Most of the unemployed have fled these rural settings for the cities. Those left behind have little to do and set a slow pace in the forsaken place.

So the town houses the compound. The compound houses the room. And the room houses the . . . cupboard. Now I can hear the low hum of hymns emerging from the cupboard. That's because if you open the cupboard and remove the bottom board, you'll find an opening that descends to an underground illegal Chinese house church. It's in this secret place that eighty-odd Chinese Christians are huddled together, breaking the law by reciting psalms from their smuggled Bibles, hailing Jesus and shouting hallelujahs. To be a member of such a church is to violate the law, be a political criminal, and risk persecution, potential prison, and perhaps worse. But then, like many before them, they are crusaders—out to spread the word by whatever means necessary.

Me . . . I am just a reporter, here to document their story. For eleven hours we have observed and witnessed what it's like to be a believer on the run. My crew and I had arrived at one in the morning under the cover of darkness so as to avoid detection from ever-suspicious neighbors. During the morning tour of the compound—the simple kitchen, the horrifying bathrooms, and the claustrophobic sleeping quarters—we were shuttled around hurriedly, not permitted to stand in the open courtyard for fear that those same neighbors' watchful eyes would catch a glimpse of us.

Now I've been stowed away, hidden in the darkness because of a simple knock on the main door. Should the police show up and catch us—cameras in hand—the very best we could hope for is a simple arrest and speedy deportation. Our hosts will be sent to jail.

But it's just a false alarm (the third one this morning). We can now carry on with our well-choreographed departure strategy. Within moments the three of us—myself and my two colleagues—will be scuttled from the compound through the back door, one by one, like a hostage from a safe house to a waiting van that will charge from the clearing, slip and slide through the muddy road until we are safely out of sight.

On the road from Guangzhou, China, to the underground house church, there's one particularly curious stretch. On either side of the broad highway there are small, one-story buildings. Each of their doorways is lit up with holiday colored lightbulbs, as if the same wandering salesman outfitted the entire town. Directly in front of the doorways are young girls—dressed in tight red coats and formfitting jeans. As each car or truck (it's mostly a trucking route, and each and every blue truck looks identical) pulls through, the girls run forward, waving their hands, beckoning the driver and passengers, smiling, and soliciting business. A number of these blue trucks are lined up in front of the buildings. Their cabins are empty—the drivers nowhere to be seen.

To understand how these three scenes are related, we have to look both forward and backward.

Fifty years of Communist domination—thirty years of the cultural revolution, during which China's regal past was laid to waste, and twenty years of its legacy—have produced a fairly spiritually naked landscape. Today, various faiths—Christian revivalism among them—are on the rise. Still, there is resistance. The Chinese government monitors religious activity, and any organization that operates outside of that supervision is considered illegal, branded a cult, its members considered criminals. Much of their literature—some versions of the Bible included—are also considered illegal and therefore need to be smuggled into the country. You can't use the post office for these operations because, as in our country, the federal government oversees these postal routes and facilities. In addition, the Chinese authorities also allegedly monitor underground Christians and catch them should they come to a post office to receive an illegal package. So, smugglers have started to use private shipping—boxes and crates full of illegal Bibles stuffed into the cargoes of the countless blue trucks that streak across the Chinese countryside. While it would be easy enough for the Chinese government to disrupt this trade as well, they won't, because private shipping is a commercial activity. It's good for the economy, and if there's one ideology that the Chinese government has faith in, it's the mighty buck. In other words, they're willing to trade a Bible for a buck.

Now, of course it's the drivers of these infamous blue trucks and their precious cargo that are making regular stopovers at the eccentric brothels hosted by the red army girls. Most often, they do their thing, slurp some noodles, drop some bills, and are off in the course of maybe an hour. But it's not uncommon that they'll take something other than a satisfied smile with them on their way. That is, as in other developing nations all around the world, HIV infection is up in China. And one of the main reasons for its rapid spread is these truckers.

In essence, these guys are both sinners and sanctifiers, crisscrossing China, spreading both the gospel and AIDS. They are the drivers of this drama in more ways than one. They are the actual drivers behind China's brewing private commercialization. They are smugglers responsible for China's rapid spiritualization. They are the viral carrier of China's potentially worst epidemic outbreak. And they play out the majority of those roles completely unbeknownst to themselves. And, in fact, often it's the anonymous characters of the universe who are most responsible for how we as a people proceed.

Dr. Johnathan Chen (I've changed his name for his own safety)—the sixtysomething missionary who has for decades repeatedly risked arrest to make illegal trips to work with the underground churches in China and who served as our own escort through the interior of China—sees it this way:

"The road to deliverance is never a straight path. It travels in strange circles."

In what we have seen the last few days, this is most certainly accurate—old men walking backward, secret hideaways full of devoted pilgrims, roads traveled by sinners and saints.

Dr. Chen is a missionary in the old school way—traveling in secret, enduring the harshest of conditions under the ubiquitous threat of persecution—Bible in hand and gospel in spirit because something in his soul propels him. Ideologically speaking, I am quite sure that I don't agree with him and his crusade to convert "nonbelievers" everywhere into Christ-loving souls. Yet something about his determination inspires me and makes me want to keep up with him.

It's not until our final day together—the ninth one spent on the road—that something Dr. Chen says resonates with some of my own inner determination.

"Every believer has a story. I quite like meeting the stranger out in the countryside who has struggled all his life—who has made it through poverty, famine, the revolution, and Mao—and now has found freedom in his faith. I feel I am not his teacher, but that he is mine."

I think Dr. Chen is right. Most of us believe in something even if it's the conviction that we'll never believe in anything at all. Either way, the people we meet along the way, the strangers interloping along these long learning highways, show us new things, remind us of old things, and keep the journey intriguing.

Dr. Chen is a preacher. He likes to use these words—belief, faith, and freedom. They are familiar ones and will be explored throughout this text along with others. But as the

American poet T. S. Eliot once said, ". . . the end of all our exploring / Will be to arrive where we started / And know the place for the first time."

It seems to me, then, that if the destination is not something new but just a new way of looking at the world, then the old man walking backward in Guangzhou has already arrived there. He sees the world from a unique angle, at a certain pace, and, one assumes, it passes him by in a very "different" way from what you or I might experience. To me he's a symbol of someplace I'd like to arrive.

Dream-weavers

Fate

On December 24, 1999, a lesser heralded hijacking took place aboard an Indian Airlines plane that originated in Katmandu, the capital city of Nepal, and was destined for New Delhi, India's capital city. At first, the media rushed to the story—it was a mere week before the new year, and news all around the world was abuzz with the potential terror that threatened to wreak havoc during the many planned new year's millennial celebrations. However, it soon became clear that this hijacking had little to do with the new year or whatever other symbolic portents it might represent or could potentially bring about, but rather was concentrated on regional politics in northern India. Within twenty-four hours of the occupation of the plane, an Islamic fundamentalist group claimed responsibility for the hijacking, and shortly thereafter they made their demands. They insisted on the release of a Muslim cleric imprisoned in India, along with a number of "freedom fighters."

Since 1948, Kashmiri secessionists have supported an independence movement that in the past decade has turned violent and deadly. Along with the Palestinian struggle, Kashmir has become a flashpoint for Islamic fundamentalist grievances against the western world. Kashmir makes up a northern region in India, the control of which has been hotly disputed between India and Pakistan for over fifty years. The predominant faith in Kashmir is Islam, as it is in Pakistan, and as a result, Muslims from all over the world—especially Kashmir itself, Pakistan, and Afghanistan—have adopted the freedom movement as a *jihad,* or "holy war." I was familiar with the conflict taking place in Kashmir, since I had spent some time covering the story for Channel One just a few months before.

Of course, no one could predict that the events unfolding in 1999 would so profoundly portent the violent hijackings that would take place less than two years later on 9/11/2001. Like so many other international news stories, this hijacking story slowly faded from the headlines of American news networks.

By Christmas Day, the plane had landed in Amritsar, India; Lahore, Pakistan; and Dubai in the United Arab Emirates, before finally resting atop the tarmac in Kandahar, Afghanistan. And when the first hostages were released—twenty-seven women and children—grisly details began to emerge. The group of hijackers, five young men, had boarded the plane fully equipped with hand grenades, guns, and knives. About forty minutes into the flight from the beautiful foothills of the Himalayas in Nepal they had seized control of the aircraft and forced the pilot to alter the flight course. Among the original 178 passengers and crew on board the plane were a number of young honeymooners. At least one young man—a twenty-seven-year-old honeymooner himself—had been stabbed to death when he disobeyed an order by one of the hijackers not to look directly at him. As happens with many of these terrorist seizures, this situation unwound into protracted media discussions about regional politics, national grudge matches, and international rules of terrorist protocol. By the day after Christmas, the story had become a lingering update amid headlines that were once again focusing on new year's preparations—terrorist threats and all. The chance of any deeper message emerging from the still-pending outcome of the hijacking seemed lost.

I found my holiday spirit dampened by all of the above. A week earlier, the *Los Angeles Times* had asked me to write a very brief "millennium wish," a few words in which I would articulate my wish for the next millennium. I supposed they wanted something optimistic and hopeful, yet watching all these aforementioned events on my television, I felt depressed and cynical. I resolved that my one wish was for all of us, collectively, as a species, was to find a way to escape this "tribal" mentality—this primitive, barbaric behavior where we kill one another over disputes of land and ideas. In all honesty I wasn't convinced there was much hope of it coming true.

One night after the latest CNN update, during which nothing much had changed aboard the plane, I clicked off the television, sat in my kitchen, and thought about what was happening halfway across the world. I found my thoughts wandering the way of the young man who had been killed. At twenty-seven years old, he was hardly much older than I was. Presumably, he had gone to Nepal with his new bride for a few days, excited about the life ahead of them both, bracing for the mystery of a new and long life they would spend together. And now he was returning in a body bag, stabbed to death in front of his wife because he had dared to stare a terrorist in the eyes. Some would say such are the wheels of karma. Somehow that didn't sit well with me. How would the cliché read in a case like this? Fate works not only in mysterious ways, but in terribly tragic ones as well. At the time, I was contemplating this book—how I might write it and what were the components that would go into it. I had collected a number of texts on the life of the Buddha and some of the teachings he had produced during the course of his life. I tried for a few moments to come up with some suitable explanation—some sort of cosmic spiritual law or simple phrase or fragment that justified what on the surface was nothing more than cruel bad luck. I waited and hoped secretly that I was on the threshold of some major revelation.

Nothing.

Instead, I found that I was becoming increasingly agitated at the thought of the hijacking—and, more to the point, the hijackers. Who the hell were these terrorists that they thought they could recklessly impede on others' lives, steal a future from an innocent stranger? Like many others around the world, I was sick of terrorists, who because of their fanatical beliefs in their narrow versions of God felt they had the right to terrorize the rest of us. And with new year's fast approaching, the world itself was bracing for what seemed an almost obligatory terrorist strike. Every news outlet—from local to national to international broadcasts—was full of stories about antiterrorist precautionary preparations. The world itself was rooted in fear, armed and poised for an inevitable apocalypse. Where, I wondered, had we managed to steer ourselves? Frustrated and fatigued, I flipped my book over and decided to meditate in hopes of quelling my emotions. As occurs rather often, I soon drifted into sleep.

Fuzz

At first the image is murky, and it takes me a few moments to figure out where exactly I am. But soon the familiar low hum of plane engines and the discomfort of the condensed seat alert me to the fact that I am sitting aboard an airplane. I look around, and the brown complexions of the passengers plus the dilapidated interior of the cabin soon convey to me that I am most likely aboard a plane in India. Having traveled extensively through much of the country, I know there is no mistaking this scene or, unfortunately, this smell. No sooner have I arrived at this revelation than I hear a cry emerge from the rear of the airplane. After the first cry, a succession of panicked shrieks and shouts rage throughout the cabin. Amid the chaos, a man charges into the front section of the plane where I am sitting. He is cradling a Kalashnikov AK-47 machine gun in his hands and shouting in a language that I can't really make out. Upon seeing this, I feel a surge in my stomach. And then as I rise—not yet knowing the reason why—I find that beneath my own oversize sweatshirt is a rusted, black, metallic automatic weapon. And as soon as I reveal it, the horrific shrieks around me intensify. I have introduced another element of terror into the equation. My heart is racing as adrenaline pumps through my whole being.

My head is loud with words and flooded with questions. *What's going on? Why am I with them—the terrorists? Why the hell am I carrying a weapon?* But I am without answers, caged by my own terror and uncertainty over what exactly is going on. But then clarity comes. I *am* with them. I have hijacked a plane, imposed terror on its occupants, and cast myself in a horrible drama. At a subtle level I know that I detest my own actions, that I loathe terrorists, who bring about terror to innocents because of their self-righteous and primitive beliefs. But now I am driven by my own fear, my own lack of control or ability to impose order. I am helpless, wielding a weapon of killing in my hands in order to force my will. This is what I have been reduced to. I look into the eyes of a young woman in front of me, staring at me in my confused frenzy. The fear in her eyes is clear. She sits at the other end of my weapon, waiting for me, or perhaps some greater force, to determine which course fate shall follow. But I don't know what I want, so her innocent stare cripples me and makes me shake with my own fear and now quickly evolving anger.

There are five of us including me, holding guns, shouting like madmen, generally terrorizing. One of the gang has gone to the cockpit. He's forcing the plane wherever it is that he wants it to go.

But now my bolder self steps forward and seizes control. My emotions are hot. I turn the gun on my mates—the other terrorists gripping their guns tightly. I am overcome by my anger, my distaste for these horrible young men. I'd like to do nothing other than unload a stream of bullets, tear them apart, and eradicate their threat.

Their eyes are full of fear and uncertainty. *Will I really do it?* They're not sure, and neither am I. I am dubious, because something tells me that that would hardly solve the problem or make the fear and anger go away. But I'm not keen on letting go of this impulse to kill these terrorists. Our journey, this wild dream, has now reached a new, critical level of intensity in that someone soon will surely crack and the guns will start popping.

Except that all of a sudden things start to fade. The noise from the plane dissipates and the sound of the engines lulls. The craziness dies away, and slowly so do the faces; one by one, all of the passengers as well as the militants disappear, until finally the cabin of the plane is warm and silent and only one passenger besides me is left. He is sitting in row 6, seat C, on the aisle. I look at him. His face is calm. His eyes are soft, and his demeanor carries with it a forceful peace. I am not sure how to describe him—what I can say about his bearing except that he is not afraid. The transformation in mood has made me anxious, yet just looking at his still face, I find my emotions receding like the tide of the ocean. As I look at him from top to bottom, I can see that he's wearing only an orange robe that drops over his narrow shoulders. He is clearly the classic image of a Tibetan monk.

Unsure of what to say, I find that I am silent, waiting, trusting that things are as they should be.

But soon questions flood my head. *Where are we? Where are we going? Why am I here?*

He answers.

Where are we? In the midst of this dream world, we are aboard a plane—a metaphorical carrier that cruises across time and space. It is a movement that does not stop. It is a movement unafraid of the past or the future, it is simply rooted in the constant unfolding of the present. It moves without doubt because that is all it knows how to do.

Where are we going? In front of us there is an infinity of destinations, the final one to be determined by the course we decide upon now. This is the matrix of time, a convoluted collection of time strands in a universe of infinite possibilities.

And why are you here? Because up until now, you have always been fixed on the future, unaware that it's the present that dictates fate. To be released from the chains of the past and the future is to find freedom.

And freedom is where it is.

This man's answers come simply from him, his manner is effortless. I must admit that to me his words don't immediately make sense. They don't solve the riddles of life. Yet I do have the distinct and familiar impression that the meaning of these words lurks not just in the study of them, but in my own experience.

So here we are aboard this plane all by ourselves. The cockpit is now empty, and the craft is flying all on its own toward an uncharted place—destination unknown.

Together we sit, amid the silence, on our voyage to a place I don't know. Soon I know that he will fade away as well and I will be alone, on a solitary journey. For I have discerned that the trail to freedom is one that must be walked alone. The journey of the self is meant to be one traveled only by the self and no other. "This," he tells me, "is the one true fate that there is."

Fade out.

The following day, while driving to the airport to pick up a family member, parts of my dream started to pop back into my head. Like disjointed scenes from a movie, the images bob up from my subconscious. As one leads to another, I try to piece them together in a sequential order that might restore some meaning. And slowly I start to realize that will not happen.

I resolve to let go, not to try to put together the puzzle with the absence of so many pieces. Surely the meaning of my subconscious encounter is lurking somewhere, and I trust it will creep up on me, most likely at some unexpected time. Terrorists and a monk aboard a lonely, lost plane—one can only wait for things to reveal themselves.

On December 31, 1999, New Year's Eve, the ordeal aboard the Indian Airlines A300 Airbus came to an end. In the end, no more hostages lost their lives. In fact, the images of the hostages reuniting with their families just hours before the crisscrossing of millenniums in New Delhi provided some powerful imagery to a world that had gotten caught up in the technological game of the imminent twenty-first century. Newscasters read buoyant scripts to flickering images of teary hostages hugging their relatives in New Delhi's Indira Gandhi International terminal— scripted happy endings to a weeklong drama that included all the must-have elements: masked marauders, innocent victims, heroes, villains, and timeliness. The hijackers had managed to broker a deal. Three prisoners were released from jails in India along with the requested cleric. The hijackers disembarked the plane, were granted an allotted time to disappear, and did so successfully, but not before one of them announced to the exhausted hostages, "You'll see us again." (Perhaps one day we will know the whole horrifying truth of those words, since as of the publication date of this book authorities had not yet publicly solidified the suspicions that these same masked terrorists may have played a role in the events of September 11, 2001.) Still, at the time the story seemed to have found a strange but suitable ending.

Soon, the celebration and fireworks all around the world overtook the headlines. The hijackers disappeared, and the story of the hijacking faded away into the archives as a news tidbit that had provided some brief excitement, but little else. But for me, though I was physically half a world away, without anyone I knew in a personal way aboard the plane, the story had had a very strong effect. Perhaps it was because I could not find any sense to explain what it was that had taken place—why a young man of twenty-seven had been killed and why my own dreams had been invaded by these incidents. I kept thinking about it, over and over again, trying to figure out how what had gone on aboard that plane had crossed over into my own subconscious. And I kept returning to the word that the man had left me in my dream: *fate.*

Fate is a very curious thing. Most of us are familiar with the expression "You reap what you sow" or "What goes around comes around." But many of us also know that these sorts of simple equations don't always apply when it comes to real life. In other words, sometimes you do indeed reap what you sow. At other times, however, you sow, sow, sow, and don't reap much of anything at all. And often you or someone you know is that lucky star who hasn't sown a single seed but reaps the farm. It's difficult to believe that a young man on the way back from his honeymoon, sitting beside his new bride, somehow deserves to be murdered by a group of fanatical thugs. It defies logic. It defies any supposed cosmic code of morality—why do good people suffer or sometimes even die untimely deaths?

Suffering. It's a term that is quite central in Buddhism and lies at the core of the Buddha's life journey. Very simply put, Buddha's self-proclaimed purpose in life was to solve the riddle of life, to understand why suffering exists in human life at all and how to get rid of it. Buddha's trail is one that is based in reality but also crosses easily into mythology. Like all the great prophets—Moses, Jesus, Mohammed, and Krishna, to name a few, Buddha's legend is one that has become symbolic in its retelling. Indeed, it blurs the line from the "real" world that exists in front of us and the dream one that lurks in our subconscious. Buddha's trail is an enduring one because it includes all the elements of the traditional spiritual journey. His story is a simple one—it is about a young man who goes from prince to pauper to finding true power. But his story, like all good ones, starts at an unlikely place, at a time before even he was born. It starts with that esoteric term—*fate*.

She had a dream beneath a tree, on her way home to give birth to a boy who would change the world. In fact, some accounts discount that it was a dream at all. Either way, if the following was based in the physical world or the dream one, it hardly seems to matter.

The garden itself was rich with texture. The trees were green. The streams sparkled like diamonds. The cool wind breezed through like a whisper.

Amid a garden so lavish that it clearly resembled the heralded Garden of Eden, Queen Maya, who as tradition dictated was traveling from the royal kingdom to her maiden home to give birth, stopped over and had a vision. In it, she reached to a tree and plucked a branch. As she did, she simultaneously delivered an infant boy. But this was hardly a normal child. For very quickly, the Hindu gods descended from the heavens to witness the baby rise up and take seven steps in every direction. He also declared, "I alone am honored, in heaven and on earth." The queen in great excitement reported the series of events to the king, who could not have been more thrilled that his heir had performed such extraordinary feats.

When a newborn stands up and walks in seven steps in all directions, surely something is up—any 1-900-PROPHET could tell you that. Accordingly, as was custom, the king reported the visions to his courtiers, several of whom specialized in reading fortunes as well as the stars. In the kingdom there was great rejoicing, for the promise of a great future leader ensured a level of prosperity that was worth getting worked up about.

When told the story of the infant prince's birth, the dream-readers turned powerfully contemplative. They didn't bother to consult one another but sat instead silently, each of them breaking it down individually.

Finally, after what seemed an eternity, the first wise man began to nod slowly. "You have brought into this world a great leader." A collective sigh emerged. There must have been giddy whispers from all in the room. "But," the second wise man interrupted. "Which kingdom will he rule?"

Beautiful—every oracle must have his day. Confusion reigned, and more hushed whispers whipped around the room. Both the king and queen had strained expressions, unsure of the meaning of these words from the second wise man. However, they knew better than to intrude with a question. The nature of these inquiries was that *what was said was said* and no exploratory answers were given. The finality lay with the third wise man. Finally he lifted his head and stared straight ahead.

"A leader can take charge only of what he knows." He spread his hands not far apart from each other. "Within these walls lies a world. Beyond these walls lies another world. And beyond the boundaries of the kingdom lies still another world. Whichever the boy chooses he shall lead. Whichever definition of power he seeks he shall have. That is his fate."

Great . . . fantastic . . . wonderful. Fortunes are such that they often serve only to confuse life some more. But who wants to know the end of the movie before the beginning, anyway? Who except those conspiracy theorist freaks and paranoids reads the last page of a book before they read the first page? Alas—many of us do indeed fall into that category—many of us would love to know how it's all going to shake out. We like to believe that we are the authors of our own scripts, but as evidenced by the plethora and popularity of star-readers, palm-readers, 1-900-PROPHETS, and other registered "futurists," many of us also have some sneaking suspicion that some other force may be at work.

Prince Siddhartha's prophecy is no less circular. And so it is that the Buddha's life is launched by the hands of fate. But that fate is uncertain, lying in wait for the forces of time and the power of intention to trigger its eventual fruition. For Buddha this then is the machine behind the passage of time—a creaking cosmic clock that ticks away while life works its way out.

But for most of us moderners, the idea of fate hampers us because its very definition dictates that whatever lies in the future is unavoidable. Eastern traditions at a very subtle level have managed to circumvent this definition and to suggest that fate is simply the evasive outcome, not predisposed but determined, by active choice making in our lives. The myth behind Buddha's birth and prophecy is a clear symbol of that. The routine plays itself out—the auspicious birth, followed by the perplexing prophecy, all leading up to . . . the unfolding of a life. Ultimately no matter what the fates say, a lifetime needs to be lived out. It's an insurance salesman's credo—nothing is for certain until it all shakes out—*so get your game on.*

"The only certainty there is is uncertainty," a seventeen-year-old young man named Payham told me when I was in Iran a few years ago. We were hanging out at a pizza place on a Friday night among a crowd of teenagers; an unlikely scene in Iran the past two decades but one that has reemerged in the last few years. In supersecret moments Payham might reach out and touch his girlfriend, a quick grip of her hand or soft brush of her cheek. They, like all unmarried couples, had to be careful not to be seen by the Islamic secret police called the *Basiji,* who enforce rigid Islamic laws prohibiting displays of affection between the sexes.

At one point his hand must have lingered too long or his glance shown too much affection because a member of the *Basiji* came up to us. He had a machine gun strapped to his back.

"May I help you?" Payham asked him in his native tongue when the *Basiji* came over.

The man barked a few words gruffly and Payham responded calmly.

The whole encounter lasted only a few minutes. Finally the *Basiji* walked away, and I asked what happened.

"He told me to be careful, not to get too close." Payham nudged his girlfriend playfully. "I asked him what he meant, and he said I knew what he meant."

Payham shook his head. "But really it's too much of a pain for him to arrest me or take me away. He'd rather roam the street with his gun and wave it around now and then, than deal with one little punk like me."

"Aren't you afraid?" I asked, having heard so many stories about what some of these thugs have done to young men for violating these stupid rules.

"You know, here in Iran, you cross paths with these guys all the time. You say things maybe you shouldn't, and sometimes you get away with it. I guess I know better than him that things here are going to change soon."

Payham took his girlfriend's hand in his and smiled sweetly at her. It was a simple fleeting act, one of powerful defiance, and I hoped to myself that Payham would soon win over the *Basijis.* We'll see what is fated, I said.

Payham shook his head. "I don't think I'll leave it to fate. Fate is not so certain. The only certainty is uncertainty."

I had fallen into a familiar trap. It's too easy to think of fate as a force out there just lurking, stalking us and waiting to make a dramatic, if not surprise, appearance. But sometimes life intrudes and throws that logic to the wind.

I once consulted a New York City cabdriver on these quandaries. We were jammed on the Brooklyn-Queens Expressway on the way to John F. Kennedy Airport, where I was supposed to catch a flight. It was apparent that I was going to miss it. Lev, my Russian, intellectually inclined taxi driver, shrugged. "It's fated for you to miss it." I'll save you all the pretext, but when I questioned his definition of fate—why some arbitrary force or God would want me to go through the headache of a missed flight—Lev smiled and shook his head.

"No, no, no, it's not some silly thing like the plane crashes and we all say hallelujahs that you weren't fated to die on that plane." Lev shook his head and didn't bother to look back at me. "It's simply that you booked a flight at a shitty time, in the middle of rush hour, left your place too late, and brought this on yourself. You generate a certain fate for yourself, brother. Fate isn't some external absolutism that is imposed on you. It's all about you, my man, the choices that you make that bring you to this moment."

There you are. This is the enduring fate as presented in Buddha's birthing story; fate should propel us not to an indifferent world of determinism, but rather to an empowered sense of authority.

The series of events that took place aboard that Indian Airlines jet between the week of December 24 and December 31 led to a series of more *fateful* events. That should hardly surprise us when we come to understand that every choice we make mobilizes a certain outcome, a certain *fate,* if you will. Be they individual choices, the consequences can have collective effects.

The hijackers had ordered the passengers not to make eye contact with them. When one young man did, he paid for it with his life. Why, I wondered, was it that the hijackers were afraid of someone looking into their eyes? Were they simply afraid of being recognized? They were already masking their faces with bandannas. Or was it something else? Perhaps they were afraid of what the passengers would see? Would they see fear and terror in the eyes of the terrorists, the men with guns, who were too afraid of a world where they couldn't find answers? Were the terrorists as afraid as any of their captives?

Mixing the images and emotions from my dreams, I started to think that maybe that was indeed part of it—the hijackers were as fearful and confused about their lives as any of the innocent victims they were terrorizing. They were acting from a place of desperation and fear. They, along with all of us, were in the midst of some lonely journey, trying to wade through the mismatched moments of life, searching for whatever it is that is waiting for each of us to materialize. This time, their actions had triggered the unfolding of a story that would culminate in an infinite number of ways.

The three prisoners and the Muslim cleric released as part of the deal would certainly find that their lives would spin into some unexpected ways. Within a week, one of the released "freedom fighters" was leading anti-American and anti-Indian demonstrations in the Pakistani city of Karachi, pledging to destroy these "satanic" nations, promises more eerie now so many years later. The released prisoners would bear the legacy of a truly traumatic experience, one in particular: the widow of the murdered passenger would be forced into an entirely unexpected new future.

And I myself found that the whole drama half a world away had triggered something in me—a subconscious encounter with a dreamy prophet that promised to show me how his story resonated with my world. And you, too, are part of this play. Because you're on your journey, too—that's the way fate works.

Forest-walkers

Days spilled into weeks, then months, and eventually to years.
Young Buddha—going by his given name of Siddhartha—
grew up royally within the palace walls. Every so often—in as
controlled a circumstance as possible—the prince was escorted
outside of the palace through the city streets and the sur-
rounding forests. On one such trip, from his royal carriage the
young prince saw four sights: an old man, a dying man, a dead
man, and a monk. Having never before seen such things, he was
struck by the horror of age, disease, death, and the marked sim-
plicity of the monk, who seemed not bothered at all by the in-
evitability of these life stages. Siddhartha wondered to
himself: Are all men destined to endure this same path? To see
their youth fade into age, sickness, and eventual death? Or is
there a possible reprieve? Unable to summon an answer despite
his supreme education, the prince grew fearful and quickly re-
turned within the safety of the palace walls.

Fear

Today, dream-readers take out ads in city newspapers. They're squeezed in between lusty-looking girls and personal ads, and their 1-900 services come with a seventy-five-cent service charge. Quite often their advice is generic, resembling the broad wisdom of a fortune cookie. And in fact, the tradition of fortune-telling and dream-reading hasn't changed all that much since ancient times. In other words, the mutability of the dream world and its analysis remains intact. In Buddha's case, the prophecy, like most prophecies, was ambiguous—the type of declaration that could be twisted any number of ways to mean any number of things. But then again, many of us are willing to roll the dice anyway, to latch on to the yarn of an anonymous stargazer, a Lower East Side tarot card reader, or some *I Ching* Internet server based out of Orange County.

Do we believe in the predictions these messengers bring to us? Do we truly think that in their spare time, these eccentric oracles hang out on the other side in some sort of live-wire world where information archives on all of us are logged? Why do we long for some secret remedy for our anxieties? And is there a deeper worry, a more profound anxiety about the absence of anything to assure us?

Sometimes the only way to find out is to step into the unknown.

"You can see some pretty horrible stuff out here."

"Like what?" I said reflexively, and then cringed the moment I said it. War is easier when the details are absent.

"You see young boys dying." There was a pause from the young commander now as he looked at me confidently. "And that's not the worst of it. Because we are soldiers and we know that that may happen to any of us at any time. We're prepared for that."

We walked a few yards through the woodsy terrain, I, gripping a handheld microphone hardwired into the video camera following us, he with a Kalashnikov AK-47 automatic weapon held loosely at his side.

"Death does not scare us so much as . . ." He stopped. We were two twentysomething guys who under different circumstances, on another night half a world away, might have been walking through Washington Square in New York City in search of a late-night meal. Instead, this dank, cold afternoon, we were searching through the Kashmiri hills of India for armed militants hidden in woodsy enclaves. "For us, the fear lies in that death is hiding in these hills waiting for us. We don't know which tree he's hiding behind, when he'll come, how fast he'll come, and probably most terrifying, *why* he'll come for us."

Before I could take in these dramatic words, a whistle shrieked from in front of us.

The commander barked an order in Hindi and quickly gestured to me, hissing, "Get down, get down."

I knelt down and then followed the example of Major Khan, ducking my head until my chin almost touched the wet grass.

Twenty young soldiers, spread out in a radius of a hundred yards all around us, fell onto their chests, their guns propped and aimed straight ahead. All of them squinted through their sniper lenses, intensely scanning the surrounding hillsides. For the next few minutes, the only sound I could hear was heavy, nervous breathing—mostly my own. I craned my neck and looked behind us, through the drizzle and mist curling around the giant trees all up the hillside. Twenty-five yards to our rear, crouched behind a tree, one of the young soldiers had a rocket launcher poised on his shoulder as he pivoted his head, searching for the slightest movement among the trees. His responsibility was to guard our tail from a surprise attack. In the front of the battalion, beyond where I could see, another boy did the same—protecting the head of our unit from a militant siege. The initial whistle had come from a scout—the least enviable and most courageous position of the whole unit—one of two young soldiers who runs ahead of the whole unit in order to scope out the terrain and, as the commander put it, "if need be, draw fire."

My anxiety dissipated within the first ten minutes of lying down on the wet grass. I could sense no imminent threat, and I soon found myself calculating the amount of time it would take us to get back to our hotel, and what I would order for dinner once we got there. After still another twenty minutes of silence and intense concentration on behalf of the soldiers, the order came from our commander to get up and resume walking. Without a word, the soldiers climbed to their feet, hoisted their weapons, and once more started their solemn march.

Mitchell Koss, my producer and cameraman, and I had been invited by the Indian army to go out on an "anti-insurgent patrol" in the Kashmiri hills. Kashmir is a mountainous region in northern India, control of which has been hotly contested by India and Pakistan for the past fifty-two years, since the two nations' formal partition. Today, in the dense, hilly regions covered by trees and frost, Islamic "militants" or "freedom fighters" (depending on which political spin you subscribe to) are battling the Indian army, often collecting weapons, hiding in the hills and local villages, and intermittently participating in surprise attacks of resistance against Indian rule. Over the past ten years of armed conflict in the region, tens of thousands of soldiers, militants, and citizens have been killed in this hidden war that rarely seems to make its way into the world's newspapers. Mitch and I had ventured north to some of the foothills where the fighting was not overly intense to get a feeling of what exactly it was the rest of the world was missing out on. Today was preparation for the following day, for which we had planned an excursion even farther north, where regular confrontations with the insurgents occurred.

We had hooked up in Srinagar (Kashmir's capital) with the army's public relations officer, Major R. K. Purshottam, who had arranged this jaunt for us—a three-hour drive from the capital city on the sole road guarded by the Indian army from attack.

It had been over a half hour since the commander's dramatic declaration about the soldiers' fear of death, but his words were still swimming in my head. So I asked him to elaborate.

"You see, we know that our cause is just." Then he recited what, to me, seemed like the standard soldier rhetoric about the nobility of their mission, their killing being in the name of some larger cause and fate. It was the type of disclaimer reminiscent of war biographies, Hemingway novels, or Hollywood war movies—that killing in the midst of war is a fact and even denotes a certain triumphant heroism.

"But when you're out here in these woods, you sometimes forget what it is you are fighting for. And every once in a while, you run into the enemy out here and you see his eyes—either before you kill him or afterward, and looking closely, you realize he's just like you. He's cold and hungry and afraid and confused. Back at the base or better yet in the cities, you don't have to think about these things. But this world out here in the woods, wandering around with guns—this is the real world, and every once in a while when you're alone you just have to face it. Out here in the woods, there are many questions and sometimes few answers."

I nodded, unsure that I had any "journalistic" type of response adequate for what he had just said.

He barked another order to the troops, and in a few moments we had turned around and were trudging back toward the base camp.

Despite the darker realities lurking in the immediate countryside, the army base camp at Pelgaham is actually a charming little place. It sits on a guarded hillside and overlooks the bustling city down below. The city of Pelgaham is well known to most Hindus, as it is one of the gateways for Hindu pilgrims starting out on their ascent to Amernath—an ancient devotional site for the Hindu god Shiva. On the main street and along most of the narrow alleyways that branch off of it, countless merchants squat, peddling thousands of trinkets, travel tools, snacks, beverages, and devotional accessories that every pilgrim "must have." The main street, filled with people, cars, bikes, rickshas, cows, mules, beggars, and soldiers, leads like a rushing river to a literal gateway, a cluster of tents at the base of the first hill leading up to Amernath. For the average pilgrim the journey, which can be undertaken only by foot or atop a mule, lasts about three days. Climbing the steep hillsides, the narrow paths, and often unkept trails can prove very treacherous for even expert climbers—many of whom come from the West to participate in this most "Indian" of experiences. Still, at any given time, you'll find countless Hindu devotees dressed in little more than saris or thin traditional suits, sometimes barefoot, steadfastly climbing, chanting hymns, or singing praises the entire way up. Because the journey up is truly a physical, spiritual, and psychological undertaking, the accommodations are granted no attention at all. In other words, the path to God is pretty basic—bring your own food and shelter or whatever else keeps you going. At the base of the hill, under the tents, pilgrims pause for a moment, sip hot tea, and share greasy meals and fantastic stories, either before they start their journey or as soon as they've completed it.

About twelve years earlier, during a more peaceful time in Kashmir, I had ventured with my family to Amernath. At that time we never made it farther than the base tents, as the conditions of the trail had become too treacherous and a German trekker had slipped and fallen down the steep hillside to his death. Twelve years later, the city of Pelgaham felt like an occupied territory—armed soldiers walked about and army jeeps rolled up and down the muddy roads. Still, despite the pervasive military, the pilgrims managed to generate a highly festive atmosphere. What was a bit of militancy and violence to stand between them, their god, and a wholly good time? Curious to know how all this confusion fit together, I convinced Mitch to go through some of the tents with me. Our host—Major Purshottam, the aforementioned army's PR officer—insisted that he join us. He also felt it was better that we had the presence of an officer with us, so Commander Khan and another young soldier joined us, both gripping machine guns as we wandered through the tents.

We couldn't help but draw attention to ourselves—I with my Adidas-accessorized outfit, Mitch with his giant camera, and our two armed cronies. Yet no one was intimidated by us, and within moments an enthusiastic gentleman insisted that he host us beneath his tent. He unfolded some lawn chairs, spread them out, pushed us down into them, and had hot tea and some oily biscuits brought out from behind the tent. Gradually a small group of curiosity seekers collected in our circle.

Eventually I started to ask some basic questions: Were any of the pilgrims afraid of the increased violence in the region? Would it deter them from their path? The group around us was entirely male, and their answers were determinedly fearless— even aggressive and confrontational to any potential "terrorists" out there beyond the tents. Ram, an energetic man probably in his late forties, joked out loud. "Let those terrorists come with us. We'll take them through the hills, show them our god, and everything will be all right, right? Isn't that the way it works?"

There was laughter from some of the men around us. But one man, a younger boy dressed in slim pants and a worn-out, stripped-down Puma jacket, spoke up sternly. "Those militants are bloody dogs. They're killers. They believe in nothing, so they kill for nothing. I've seen them out there." He pointed outside with his hand and scowled. "They're no better than animals." His words were ripe with anger and resentment.

Ram was undeterred. "Relax, *bahai,*" he said, addressing him with a familiar fraternal term. "Just like you've come here to believe in your god, they believe in theirs. We're all entitled and it's all the same stuff. Just out there"—he made the same gesture as the young man had moments before—"things get complicated and we lose our sense."

The words I was hearing reminded me of what Commander Khan had declared earlier, so I looked over at him, curious to see his reaction to this exchange. I was particularly curious because the moment I had met him and read the nametag stitched over his right breast, I was aware that he himself was a Muslim. The Indian army had done their job well, assigning a Muslim unit commander to lead us into the battles against their

Islamic adversaries. He kept his opinions to himself, however, smiling pleasantly and sipping his tea once in a while as the others carried the conversation.

After a few more cups of tea, we left the tent, exchanging good-luck wishes with our newfound friends for our respective journeys.

Once again alone with us, rolling along in the army jeep, Commander Khan seemed to sense that the stage was his.

"Look, those boys on the other side, they are Muslims and so am I. But I am Indian, too, and my duty is to fight them. There are other Muslims in the unit. There are Sikhs and Hindus and even some Christians in the regiment here. We fight together and we die together and we don't sit around much to think about it, because then we ask questions like the ones I mentioned to you before. I don't have answers, but because I've been out in the battlefields, I have a great many questions. But once you've seen it, there is no turning back." He paused as the jeep lurched and began the ascent back toward the base camp. "There is no turning back."

One of the most elemental parts of civilization is that no matter what sort of horrible activity is being carried on in our midst—war included—life goes on. The same way London's elite once made their way to the opera in the midst of daily bombings of the city during World War II, in Kashmir young boys will pick careful routes to avoid the violence in order to make it to a pickup cricket game. During some of our downtime in Srinagar, Mitchell and I chose to do the same.

All around India and Pakistan in hundreds of thousands of narrow alleyways, worn-out fields, and abandoned lots, millions of young boys scrape together games of cricket. The ones who attend elite schools are dressed in freshly pressed knickers and tucked-in, buttoned-down shirts, carry polished balls and bats, and wear shiny protective gear. In the slums, the boys wear tattered clothing, run around barefoot, and wave thick sticks they've crafted into bats at stripped-down balls that they'll chase down to the ends of the earth. The boys in Srinagar are somewhere in between, thrust into a city worn down by war but also financed and maintained by some of the riches that an army brings with it. On this day, about twenty boys have descended on this dusty plane and are clearly enjoying the game they are engaged in. Most of them are Muslims—this is clear by the Islamic skullcaps they wear—but not all of them.

"Krishna!" one of the Muslim boys calls out to his friend when he learns that Mitchell and I are American journalists. Krishna trots out from the middle of the field. The Muslim boy named Salim runs up beside him, playfully takes his head into a headlock, and brushes his fist into his hair. Krishna responds equally jovially and wrestles out of his friend's grip.

"So—look at us." Salim smiles at us. "Hindu and Muslim, friends and teammates." The rest of the boys in the lot roll their eyes and turn back to their game. This show of diplomacy neither surprises nor impresses them.

Though the majority of citizens in Kashmir are indeed Muslims, there are a great number of Hindus as well. And though the region is not without tension between the two, it is quite obvious that they've learned to coexist, even be friendly, as seen among the participants in this cricket game.

Salim continues unprompted. "It is very difficult when India plays Pakistan in cricket, because we do not know who to cheer for." Krishna nods in agreement—it's clear that he is the Robin to Salim's Batman in this duo. "So we just choose which players to root for."

"Along what lines?"

But Salim is too sharp to fall in this trap. "Perhaps on the battlefield it matters if you are Hindu or Muslim, but on this one we don't care."

Like most citizens of Srinagar, Salim and Krishna claim allegiance neither to India nor to Pakistan. They dream of a day when Kashmir is its own independent nation. They've made a pledge to one day vie for their own national teams so that they can take on India and Pakistan in the Cricket World Cup and finally have a team of their own to cheer for. In the meantime, though, they are content to live with the dangers of war, as long as it does not encroach upon their game or their friendship. On this field, they are fearless and the only thing that matters is the next play. Their motives and their allegiance are guided only by that. Amid the apocalypse in their midst, they've found their way.

But today, on battlefields all around the world, soldiers fighting on the front lines of war are faced with intense questions of meaning and morality. They are pushed on our behalf toward battlefields, where killing is sanctioned by the inarticulate code of war. In its midst, they confront questions about their own duty, their meaning, and their actions. And many of us, in more mundane existences, confront the same questions: Why am I here? What is my purpose? What's it all about? Often those questions come in times of peril or in the face of great danger—illness, accidents, and looming natural disasters, to name a few. But in less dramatic fashion they also emerge in the midst of the daily grind—after an eighty-hour workweek, in the middle of a six-hour exam, amid fiery arguments with lovers. These are the moments when daily life fully loses its luster and the grand design comes into question: What the hell am I doing? Why? And for what?

The truth is that today the walls of civilization feel as if they are crumbling all around us. A flip through the newspaper or a glimpse at the evening newscast is a frightening revelation into the violence and chaos engulfing our world. In the midst of all this, people today are asking questions about their roles in the world in a more probing way and at an earlier stage. We are searching for our way.

Rushing back on the wet roads from Pelgaham, Mitch, Major Purshottam, and I engaged in animated conversation, a welcome distraction from the hazard of the roads, which had become slick from the steady seasonal rains that poured down in the afternoon. It was past monsoon season, when the roads were not passable at all. Now, as the calendar pushed toward autumn and the temperature fell into frigid regions during the afternoons and nights, our driver didn't seem to pay much heed to such notions as hydroplaning or black ice. Instead, as part of the army convoy headed back for the Kashmiri capital of Srinagar, we cruised speedily on the narrow highway, dancing between bigger army trucks and jeeps carrying fatigue-covered soldiers. The commanders at Pelgaham had urged us to make our way back sooner rather than later, since the roads could not be guarded by the army at night. At intervals during our conversation, Major Purshottam would squint his eyes and carefully scan the sides of the road.

"Everything is suspicious out here. Things lurk behind the trees, over the hills, all over the place." The major echoed Commander Khan's exact words. "We stay alert. We must stay alert."

So, out of obligation, I followed the major's gaze in an attempt to see these invisible hazards at the side of the road. Yet I could see nothing out there besides the occasional wandering farmer. And in fact, I found that the green rice fields shrouded in cold mist set against a mountainous backdrop made for a rather stunning and surreal setting. Stopping for a photo was impossible, however.

Earlier in our trip, the major had informed me that the reason he didn't wear his uniform or that we didn't travel in an army jeep was that doing so made him—and us—a target for terrorists. Likewise, the reason we didn't stop for snacks, bathroom breaks, or snapshots of the stunning countryside was that it would put us at the mercy of shadowy snipers lurking along the route. "Don't bother," we were told at one point when discussing the benefits of the twenty-five-pound flak jackets we had dragged halfway across the world. "When the snipers fire, they shoot for the face."

Suddenly we found ourselves stuck in traffic caused by a landslide up ahead on the road. What had previously been a nerve-wracking dash and dance on the road had slowed to a crawl on the now mud-covered surface. Major Purshottam instructed the driver to move the car away from proximity to any of the big army trucks. He dodged my inquisitive gaze and smiled pleasantly at me when our eyes did meet, before quickly looking away. Finally he resigned himself to the fact that despite his best efforts we would not make it back to Srinagar before nightfall. Turning to Mitch and me, he motioned to the rushing river beside us.

"See there—" He pointed with a slender finger. "On the opposite bank is where they will line up."

Nervously I requested clarification.

"The militants," he replied. "By lining up on the opposite bank, they know that we cannot chase them should they fire on us. They come there with rocket launchers and machine guns and point straight here."

Soon, however, we got past the obstacle in the road and, moderately relieved, Major Purshottam urged the driver to pick up his pace. Once again we were cruising briskly in the dusk. By now, even if I was somewhat nervous, I couldn't have mustered the energy to generate a suitable fear. Instead I found that I had slowly convinced myself of the great American proclamation that "the only thing we have to fear is fear itself." Now only an hour away from our hotel, I had come to a peaceful place, gazing outside at the spectacular scenery, unafraid, even brazenly courageous, confident in the fact that war was waged mostly in secret, fearful places of the soul.

Boom!

The thundering explosion can only be described with this most cliché term. Our vehicle was just several behind a transport truck that had been hit with an explosive in the middle of the road. By the time we reached the site of the accident the overturned vehicle was a gruesome, twisted metal mess amid a military melee. Major Purshottam leapt from the car and sprinted to the scene. Officials barked loudly in Hindi, shouting orders as others raced around in confusion. Mitch and I rushed to get whatever action we could on camera. I mechanically rattled off a description of the commotion around us.

But within moments the major had rushed back toward us. With composure he alerted us to the obvious: An IED—improvised explosive device—had been set off and had flipped one of the trucks in the convoy. Three casualties were already confirmed amid the tangled wreck, and other soldiers were being tended to. Major Purshottam declared this last bit with difficulty, momentarily overcome by emotion, acutely aware that three of his "boys," as the privates were referred to, had just surrendered their lives for . . . for what? But the very next moment he regained his poise.

"You must leave the area immediately. All except armed personnel must evacuate the area *now*."

With that we were shoved into the running car and the vehicle rushed off on an unfamiliar path.

We made it back that night without any more incidents. Late that evening, tucked safely under the blankets in the room of the five-star hotel where we were the only guests, I flipped through the satellite TV channels as I tried to reconcile the day's events—marching with the patrol unit, conversing with Commander Khan, Salim and Krishna's cricket game, the men beneath the tents, Major Purshottam, and finally witnessing the horror of the violence that had taken lives. How could this world of oddity, these strange interlopers and mismatched moments all witnessed in the course of a few hours, fit together?

The following day, Mitch and I returned to the base camp just outside of Srinagar, where Major Purshottam had his office tucked in a bland one-story building just inside the guarded gates. The major briefed us on the prior day's fallout—the three young soldiers had indeed died. Several more were in critical condition. A shootout with three suspected militants had ensued—it wasn't clear who had been responsible for the detonated mine, since the Indian army shrewdly handles these matters of war and public relations with secrecy.

Late in the afternoon, as the sun was setting, Major Purshottam indulged in one of his favorite hobbies and made us tea.

"I would die for a nice cup of *chai*," the major said, smiling as he delicately handled the teacups. He seemed to know and enjoy the irony of the scene—a middle-aged army major handling delicate china and remarking about the subtle pleasure of its taste. "Here actually we call it *chai*, and it is of great frustration that others call it tea because it is Indian, and in India we call it *chai*. It's just one more thing the Brits and Americans have bumbled."

When he finished, we sipped it—lightly flavored lemon tea—and traded stories, discovering mutual acquaintances in the Indian army (my uncle had served for over twenty-five years) and theorizing about the state of global politics. All of us seemed to have reached an unspoken agreement to avoid discussing the prior day's episode. But soon the conversation slowed and an uneasy silence fell.

"Yesterday," Major Purshottam started, and then stopped, pondering his words. "I said that fear makes us alert. But fear is not just being afraid—fear is uncertainty and discontent and confusion. In safety and security, we become complacent. The war that you saw does not allow us to become complacent." He laughed softly, humbly. "It forces us to be alert."

He thought for a moment. "Sometimes the more important issue is not the fear itself—but who or what it is that you are fearing. Once you identify that, you can start the journey of discovery."

Wind Whispers

Increasingly the young prince made trips outside the palace walls, where he witnessed more poverty, suffering, and death. After every trip he'd return to the beautiful, luxurious sanctuary of the royal palace and ask his teachers—the very best in the land—why some people suffered and others lived in the lap of luxury. But none of them had a suitable answer. His feeling—that the God he prayed to was not just and fair—began to bother him. It seemed the only way not to confront these unanswerable questions was to ignore them—to follow the preset royal path before him. The king was thrilled with this turn in his son's behavior. Soon the young prince was married, and within a short time his young wife bore him a son.

Refuge

In the early autumn of 1999, I was assigned coverage of Hurricane Floyd, which was heading for the southern coast of the United States. My crew and I set out for Jacksonville, Florida, then switched our flight plans to Savannah, Georgia, and finally headed to Charleston, South Carolina, hoping we would have the good fortune of delivering ourselves directly to ground zero of the storm. Anyone who's worked in broadcast news, or simply likes to watch it, can understand the strange attraction between television news and the potential for calamity.

The day before, my crew and I had spent almost an hour in a local Wal-Mart, stocking up on a variety of supplies. I personally had loaded up on cookies, potato chips, and a wide range of beef and turkey jerkies. In addition, I purchased an entire outfit of waterproof gear—from knee-high rubber boots, to a matching Gore-Tex coat and pants, to a peculiar-looking yellow rubber hat.

At one point I found myself wandering aimlessly beside a large counter behind which hung an extended glass case full of guns. I stared at the gun rack packed with shotguns, rifles, and what appeared to my uneducated eyes to be assault weapons. In the rack straight in front of me, pistols and handguns lay on display. Having grown up in the northern part of the United States, where gun culture is far less typical, I was fascinated by the sheer number of weapons right in front of me, and I couldn't help but stare at them. As I stood there, a middle-aged burly-looking man walked up to the counter. He was dressed in an orange hunting jacket and wore a worn, brimmed John Deere cap. We exchanged nods and he introduced himself as Gus. After a moment he broke the silence.

"That one right there"—he pointed at one of the shotguns behind the glass casing—"that's the best hurricane gun."

I stared at it, confused. *Hurricane gun?* He didn't wait.

"You can saw off the barrel, right easy. And then it's an easy handle—which is what you might need."

Gus looked at me again, tilting his head inquiringly. His

expression seemed to say it all. Who was this foreign, Yankee-clad interloper? But he was also the patient type, willing to teach me.

"Around here, when a hurricane this big is coming, everything shuts down. Everybody's on their own. And when everyone's on their own, people get afraid. And when people get afraid, bad things can happen." Gus had boiled it down to an elemental equation that was hard to argue against.

For precautionary reasons, the surrounding towns and cities had all been evacuated. The restaurants, grocery stores, malls—all the things that most of us need every day had been closed because of the storm. The only people left behind were those willing to carve out some space in the absence of that structured environment and wait out the storm. Would fear arise in such a situation? I wasn't sure, since I had never really been in a major hurricane and the decision to hunker down right in the middle of one wasn't my own. My hunting-outfitted friend, Gus, had raised an interesting equation in its midst—*being alone equals being afraid.* This equation lingered in my head as we pulled our cart full of junk food, gear, and equipment to the register and checked out.

By midday we had made our way through the seaside section of Charleston. All of the storefronts and windows had been boarded up and the entire area seemed a ghost town; the only signs of life were local and national news crews buzzing like vultures around the streets, trying to scavenge the last signs of life. After doing our share of the same, we made our way to a middle school that had been converted into a shelter for towns-people to stick out the storm. By now the rain was coming down with moderate strength and the winds were gusting to just below hurricane strength. We were lucky enough to find one family of a sixteen-year-old student—A. J. Hill—who had ignored the pleas of the officials to evacuate their homes and had hunkered down in their quaint suburban residence. The official reason for their disobedience was the inability of the grandmother to get up and move anywhere with such little warning.

Along with A. J. and his grandmother were several other family members. They included A. J.'s ten-year-old brother, his seventeen-year-old cousin, Kelvin, a thirteen-year-old sister, and the two parents. All in all they seemed as if they knew the storm routine well. Among other preparations, they had stocked their fridge, loaded the freezer with all the perishable items, boarded up the windows, and removed all breakable items from the elevated cabinets. The boys were gathered around the large-screen television, playing video games, determined to play right up until the electricity went—in anticipation of which they had gathered candles, flashlights, and extra batteries. They had the volume on the television turned down so they could all take in the music playing softly on the old stereo—Al Green, followed by some Otis Redding and then Marvin Gaye, the scratched CD covers stacked on the table beside the stereo. As the rest of the family buzzed around the room, Grandma Hill sat relaxed on the couch, clutching something in her hands. I looked down to see exactly what it was that she was fiddling with and discovered that it was a string of rosary beads.

As the crew set up the lights and adjusted the furniture for the right shot, Grandma Hill waved me over and told me to have a seat beside her. She showed me the beads, fingering them delicately one at a time. We began to talk, and I asked her what she thought of the hurricane, if she had endured one before, if she was nervous.

"Not really," she responded. "God has His way of testing us."

I reminded her that this particular test was predicted to be a tempest the size of Texas—a torrent three times the size of Hurricane Andrew, which had demolished parts of Florida three years earlier and killed twenty people.

Al Green continued to wail smoothly in the background as she nodded, unperturbed. "We're good, God-fearing people. 'The Lord said, "I will blot out from the earth the human beings I have created—people together with animals and creeping things and the birds of the air, for I am sorry that I have made them." But Noah found favor in the sight of the Lord.' Genesis six, chapter seven." She smiled sweetly. "Hopefully the Lord'll look on us with favor, like He did Noah. And He'll take care of us. We'll make it through . . . God willing."

I nodded uncomfortably. I hadn't exactly packed for forty nights and forty days. I had many more questions, but I suspected I wouldn't get anywhere by asking her. She seemed the type that, though sweet on the outside, would be rather solemn in her convictions and not take well to my questioning her faith. So I repeated my questions silently in my own head. I was confused by the notion of a God who sent violent storms the way of His people. Why did He have a great need to exterminate His own children? Why did He need to test them? If He spared a chosen few, were the others less worthy of His affection and sympathy? Wasn't God supposed to be an all-merciful being? Did this God indeed judge and determine those worthy and not so worthy of His attention? Did He simply blot out the extras?

Grandma Hill started to speak again. "I know what you are thinking." She looked at me. "You're thinking that I'm nuts to believe in a God that buries His people under storms and picks and chooses who survives." She smiled. "It sounds crazy and mean, but really it's not. God's benevolence is in His giving us the strength to endure trouble like this."

She had indeed pinpointed my confusion over this vindictive, perplexing God. But her declaration had me puzzled, for it didn't fit the stereotype I had so quickly formed in my head. She wasn't just some sweet old believer who revered her Lord and Savior and surrendered herself to some abstract sense of mercy. But at the same time, she did buy into some mysterious force of protection. She was willing to give up control of her own life and that of her children and grandchildren to some scientifically unexplained, non-FDA-approved being of divinity.

Perhaps sensing my continuing confusion, Grandma Hill once again interrupted my thoughts. "Faith is the key. If you believe, then no matter what happens, no matter what, we'll all be okay. Just believe."

> *To me, God is some familiar stranger that I know that I've met before, perhaps bumped into at some odd traveling carnival, or some second-grade sushi restaurant at a local strip mall. That's the feeling that crazy drug gives me every time I take it— some hazy memory and a divinely nostalgic feeling that reminds me why I still have faith. . . .*
>
> *—An anonymous addict*

Not too long ago, I covered a piece on the reemergence of heroin as the drug of choice among American teens. We pursued all sorts of angles—hanging with customs agents down at the U.S.-Mexico border and busting mules trying to bring the drugs into the United States, going out on raids with the East L.A. sheriff's SWAT team, going into treatment centers to talk to doctors about various treatment processes. And in an effort to find a personal angle to put a face on our story, I ventured onto the Internet and posted messages on numerous Web sites that declared themselves support groups for both former users and current ones. Almost immediately I started to get replies via e-mail. There were all sorts of stories—from young runaways who had got addicted out on the street to old war veterans who had been users for over thirty years. I received notes from anonymous users just blocks from my office and bold addicts strung out in Australia. And accordingly I replied, asking questions, probing for more information, personal stories, seeking out whatever I thought might help us characterize our story.

One e-mailer in particular caught my attention. In my mind I pictured this person as a young girl—but in reality I had no idea if I was communicating with a man or a woman, young or old, because the person on the other end cautiously maintained anonymity. Our e-mail exchange carried on over a series of weeks.

I like talking to you because though I can't see you, I know you're there. You listen and you reply and you make me feel connected. . . .

Every time I received an e-mail, I would read it over several times. It made me feel good that through some invisible world I was being trusted, providing comfort, being depended on.

I would ruminate throughout the day, crafting a reply in my head before typing it on the screen, and then nervously, triumphantly punching the send button. It was a simple but strong routine—a powerful sense of connection for both of us I think, in this simple act of surrender to some mysterious stranger.

The second-to-last e-mail I ever received from my friend read like this: *Someday we'll cross paths, you and I. We'll bump grocery carts. I'll say sorry and smile pleasantly and you'll nod back. It will feel strangely familiar, and one of us may look twice, but we'll only suspect and never really know. That's the way it works. . . .*

A. J. Hill is sixteen years old. If you ask him who he is, he'll tell you his name, how old he is, who his parents are, where he goes to school, where he likes to hang out, and what some of his hobbies are—and that he's quarterback and captain of his high school football team. If you were buddies with him, he'd tell you about the perks that come with such a position in small-town U.S.A. He wouldn't be arrogant about it, but he wouldn't be too humble, either. The role has given him confidence that is easy to detect. He may tell you that a kind of celebrity status comes with being the star quarterback. That when he lines up behind center and runs the show with the emotions tied to his every move, he gets a rush that is hard for a sixteen-year-old kid to fully understand.

"It's cool, you know, that everyone trusts you to perform. I mean, they want you to do something exciting and make a good play. It's like they just depend on you." He shifts in his seat and his eyes brighten as he remembers the moment. "I mean, even at an away game when you're at the other team's home field and they're booing you, they're all still watching you, waiting for you to do something. That's just dope—it's the coolest feeling in the world. You're like the chosen one with everyone's attention on you."

A.J.'s mother interrupts us and asks him to go to the backyard, where the last few windows need to be boarded up. He nods dutifully and lays down the game controller. I volunteer to go with him.

"Check this out," A.J. says as we walk through the hallway to the back of the house. He pushes open a door. "This is my grandmother's room."

I peer inside. It is modestly furnished and spotlessly

clean—the bed made to perfection, clothes pressed and folded tightly on a chair beside the dresser.

The top of the dresser holds the only ornament of the room—a thin porcelain statue of a placid Christ figure; a traditional image of Jesus standing upright, decked in a flowing robe, with his arms by his side and one hand gently raised as if blessing some invisible disciple or group. Around the neck is another set of rosaries that flow onto the tabletop. A candle and Bible lie in the same space.

"I heard you and my grandma talking," A.J. says, and smiles. "I can play video games and do almost anything at the same time," he remarks proudly. "She's all up in that stuff. She's a believer. I just thought you might get a kick out of it." He looks at me and then nods, satisfied, and pulls the door shut, and we continue down the hall.

Outside in the backyard, the winds have died down a bit and the rains have let up, though the sky still appears gray and menacing. A.J. points at some thin wooden boards leaning up against the side of the house, and we move toward them.

I ask A.J. if he too considers himself a Christian.

"Oh yeah, sure, totally," he responds without a pause. "But just not in the way that she is—my grandma."

The first board goes up and I hold it while A.J. hammers away.

"See, I was thinking about it when you guys were talking. How can my grandma just give up and hope for the best?

"I was thinking—and I know this sounds mean and all—but maybe it's because she's older and closer to death that she figures she's got to believe in a God that controls everything so that she won't be alone."

As we continue to tighten the first board on the window, A.J. tells me about his grandfather who had died of cancer about a year and a half ago, how it was at that time that his grandma, in his words, "turned hard-core."

"I mean, I was pissed. Y'know, if God was all great, then why was He making my grandfather die . . . and suffer, too? It didn't make sense. But she just got into it even more. And I could tell, even though she wouldn't say it, it was because she was afraid. That's when she started to talk a lot about us all being God-fearing and stuff, and I just wasn't all into it. I didn't want to fear God whoever He was."

The first board is up, stuck solidly onto the side of the house. The two of us stand back and admire our work. A.J. turns to me. "And I was thinking, what kind of God leaves her all by herself like that?"

A.J.'s elder cousin Kelvin emerges through the doorway.

"Kel," A.J. looks at him and says without missing a beat, "what did you think when Grandpa died?"

Kelvin frowns and shrugs. "Sad, I guess." He shrugs again, as if he has no control over his body. "And pissed, too."

A.J. recites the same confusion to Kelvin that he has just declared to me.

Kelvin nods. "I think the thing is that as you grow up, you get so used to being around other people, you acquire more things that are yours, and all of a sudden when you get *really* old, you start to lose them."

There is a sweetness in their conception of old. I imagine that for them "old" is anything a day over thirty. While their innocence is obvious, I can't help but also notice their honesty and wisdom.

"When you start to lose things, all of a sudden you get scared, because without them, without your home and your car and your husband (and maybe your God, I think), what are you?"

A.J. cuts in. "Y'know, when I play football and I'm back

there with the ball and everyone's watching me, it's totally awesome. I mean, then I'm the one that everyone trusts and looks to."

There is a pause.

"I'm not saying I'm God or anything." A.J. grins at his cousin, knowing that he's setting himself up for ridicule. "But sometimes I wonder what will happen when it's over. I don't want to turn into one of those *Sports Illustrated* stories about some broken hero—'What happens when the cheering stops. . . .' "

The three of us laugh. Kelvin nails another board firmly over the window.

"Seriously, though, it's like this contract that we all need each other. I need them to feel good—all the people in the stands cheering for me need me to score a touchdown or something, cuz that makes them happy. That's the deal. Without each other, if you're all alone, what do you do? I mean, it's cool as long as everything goes well, but what happens when it doesn't? Then it falls apart."

There is silence as the last board goes up over the window.

We are about to go back inside when Kelvin says, "Hold on, I want to show you something."

He leads me through the now returning winds toward the garage. Darkness is descending on the deserted suburban street. Kelvin pushes the door to the garage open and the three of us enter the dilapidated interior. Bursting boxes line the walls with loose papers on their tops. A yellow bulb in the center of the ceiling sheds dim light on a small desk below. The entire garage has been converted into a makeshift office—the type that resembles one in a shipyard warehouse. After a few moments, Kelvin pulls a folder from one box and brings it over to the table.

He brushes a thin layer of dust from the tabletop with the palm of his hand. "These are some pictures of our granddad." He carefully lays four pictures side by side, and he and A.J. look at them warmly.

Grandpa Hill appears to be a tough soul with a gentle face. His frame is wiry, his face rugged, and his eyes sharp. One of the pictures captures a younger version of the man, decked out in a United States Navy uniform standing atop the tarmac of an aircraft carrier, gazing out into an infinite ocean. In his slender hands he holds a cigarette, the smoke from which glides gently, twisting into the sky. The picture has immortalized a moment—framed it in black and white for all eternity. Though his eyes are off at sea, they dance with a clear resilience and peace. There is a definite resemblance to his two grandsons in the frame of his face, the ruggedness and intensity of the brow, and the placidness of the eyes.

They look at the pictures proudly. Kelvin notices that I am focused on that one in particular.

"That's my favorite." He picks it up and flips it over on its back. Scrawled in fading pencil are a couple of lines of writing.

Take Refuge in all things of this world so that they may protect you. Be not afraid of life or anything in it as it sails by.

A.J. smiles as he reads it to himself silently. "I'm not sure I know what it means—and Kel's lying if he says he does—but it's nice. I think about it when times are tough or unclear."

Kelvin frowns at his cousin's sarcasm but nods quickly in agreement. "I think there's a lesson, and we live by it even if we're not sure how."

He pauses for a moment. "That and one other thing that we've both learned from my grandpa and this picture . . ."

The two of them looked at each other sitcom style, saying simultaneously, "Don't smoke."

Grandpa Hill had died of lung cancer.

Kelvin sweeps up the pictures and places them back in the envelope. He walks to the box from which he had lifted them and tucks the envelope securely into place. A.J. pulls the string on the light and the three of us go back inside the house. The camera crew has put together a nice little setup in the middle of the living room, and we quickly conduct an interview as conditions outside get worse and worse. This time the questions are easy and the answers as simple. We go over safety precautions and contingency plans until finally Grandma Hill closes it out. "We're all good, God-fearing folk, and faith will make it so whatever happens we'll come through." I don't know how to respond until I notice sheepish smirks spread across the faces of A.J. and Kelvin.

"Good, I think we have everything we need—thank you."

Uncertainty is the bane of all organization. Uncertainty (aka chaos) is what all of civilization fears. Uncertainty could not have been more immediate for me and my crew hidden down in a South Carolina roadside motel, waiting out Hurricane Floyd. The rains had started to fall furiously, along with the gale-force winds that had the trees swaying violently. By nine o'clock, the electricity had been knocked out and the entire motel was shrouded in darkness, save for a few rooms brightened by auxiliary power so cameras could continue to roll. Everyone in the motel, which served as makeshift media headquarters and an emergency shelter, had retreated to their rooms. The four of us in our small crew, likewise, had made our way to one of our rooms to wait out the storm in each other's company. For a while we traded stories, constantly gazing out the full-size window from our ground-floor room. The awesome power of nature was at full force, and it wasn't long until we all fell into a wondrous trance, clutching our beverages, awed by the strength of the outside world.

I reclined comfortably in a motel lounge chair, propping my feet up on the windowsill and watching the show. I had purchased at good old Wal-Mart a portable CD player and some battery-operated speakers. Nasrat Fateh Ali Khan—a late classic Sufi musician with a siren for a voice, set against simple strings and percussion, bellowed in the background. I started to think about the day that had passed, Gus in Wal-Mart, A.J., Kelvin, and their devoted grandmother. All of us now, in separate spaces, were enduring the storm—taking on a natural force that could topple us at any moment. Perhaps Wal-Mart Gus was out there clutching his gun, waiting for Armageddon to begin. And Grandma Hill, perhaps with her Bible in hand, or simply belief in her heart, also sat braced for whatever her God would bring. While the sky screamed outside, each of them had to find some form of refuge in the midst of danger.

When you strip away your address, your inheritance, your job, your diploma, your credit cards, frequent-flier packages, and your various PIN numbers, without all of those things telling you who you are, are you able to find a true identity for yourself? Are you just the projection of what you thought you were, veiled behind the masks of so many titles? Or have you built a *refuge* for yourself, a secret space of security where you don't have to confront the eternal questions of identity?

We take refuge in many things—most often simple things that we probably don't even realize conceal our identities. But as we go deeper into life, form relationships with others and the gods that we worship, we create bigger veils, more comprehensive ones, and we adopt the rituals that are prescribed by them. Grandma Hill, having been left behind by her husband of fifty years, had taken refuge in the ultimate safe space of all—that directed by her God. She had surrendered her own well-being and that of her loved ones to a force that even she couldn't fully articulate. Why? Because without that sense of protection, without that sense of security, who would look out for them? Her own grandsons understood the process. For A.J., it was exhilarating to have any attention in the course of a football game—even the enmity of opposing fans—than not to have any attention at all. Without it he was just a forsaken soldier on a battlefield strewn with countless casualties. The last salvation then becomes faith—faith in a larger system that oversees all. And in many of our heads, if you take away our beliefs—our faith either in the gods we worship or the consumer products we surround ourselves with—we are left alone.

And what happens when we are left alone? As Wal-Mart Gus would remind us, when we are alone, we become afraid.

During news events like Hurricane Floyd, the media collects at specific locales and everyone fights for space and time to narrate the same exact story. There are protocols between local and national news agencies, affiliates and freelancers, executive producers and field producers, all of which must be handled with the utmost diligence. There are hushed conversations, fierce gossip, and trade talk of the utmost acuity. And during specific hours—in a case like a hurricane, when the storm is at its peak—everyone lines up to get their shot on the satellite. A legion of reporters pass in front of the camera lens and, through various forms of verbiage, articulate the same exact thing. If you're watching at home, you're familiar with the wind-blown image of a man or woman clutching tightly to a floundering hat, holding a hand to their ear to keep their ear piece in, perhaps leaning into the wind and tearing rain. What you don't see is the "reverse angle," the world that exists on the opposite side of the lens, or for that matter outside of the frame of your own television.

In that larger reality, a hurricane serves as just another back-drop in a culture that is dependent on twenty-second sound bites and news clips to tell us what is going on with itself. In the case of Hurricane Floyd, correspondents took turns stepping outside of Room 206 at the Motel 6 by Highway 70. They were dressed to the nines in waterproof Wal-Mart gear. They screamed into a microphone while the rest of the amassed crews from all over the country waited patiently and indifferently inside Room 206, sipping warm coffee and biting into stale candy bars. Reality has become that which is projected—symbolically onto the television screens in front of us—but more specifically onto the larger screen that we've become conditioned to accept.

But the larger reality is that a greater world exists beyond the edges of these routinely ingested images of the world, and it is far more mysterious than we can imagine. In the case of an episode like Hurricane Floyd, it is far easier to see familiar images of boarded-up storefronts, closed-down roads, and wind-blown humans narrating nature's fury than to think for a moment that we even manipulate nature to serve our own sense of security. During a furious storm, most of us seek safety by fleeing from its path. Those that stay latch onto something that they hope will anchor them in the midst of the tempest—faith, belief in a cosmic order that computes all the checks and balances and can justify all possible outcomes. So while every once in a while a storm will come our way and throw us back into a heart of darkness, it is in those moments when we're stripped of all our cosmopolitan dressings that we seek safety in the last outward refuge that there is—our beliefs. It had become far too obvious to me that like Grandma Hill and Wal-Mart Gus, we too had sought refuge in common conventions that protected us from an unregulated world.

A good storm uproots trees, floods roads, flattens homes and offices as if they are nothing but some playful God's Lego land. Federal disaster funds flow, and those who survive struggle for years to rebuild lives torn apart by a few furious winds. After newscasts survey the damage, throw out wild numbers that make insurance companies cringe and construction companies tingle, life inevitably moves on without any pause at all.

For our part, a fitting end necessitated a morning-after visit to the Hill family home.

As we drove along branch-and-leaf-covered roads, carefully making our way around downed power lines and plunging our Ford Expedition into two-and-half-foot flooded potholes, I couldn't help but wonder what we'd see on the other side of the story—a family drawn together by faith that had endured the storm, or maybe one racked by the fury of some vengeful, vindictive God.

Arriving at the Hill home, we discovered Kelvin, A.J., and A.J.'s little brother in the front yard, armed with rakes and giant black plastic garbage bags. An efficient cleanup crew, the three of them vacuumed up loose leaves and thick branches that had blown all over the yard. Besides that, however, the remainder of the exterior of the house seemed intact. Indeed, A.J. reported no major ill effects from the storm. Besides one heady hour when the winds and rains picked up and slammed the outside of the house and the Hill family retreated to the sanctuary of a sheltered hallway, where Grandma Hill recited gospel (A.J. winks), the rest of the night passed relatively uneventfully.

In fact, it all had neatly wrapped together rather perfectly for Grandma Hill. Another test, another passing grade. If anything, this sort of tempestuous test had only fortified her resolve and determination to seek refuge at all opportunities. She's not open to much questioning of her faith. I'm not sure if it's because my questions undermine her beliefs (doubt it) or she simply cannot see what my angle is—why I or anyone else would even want to consider a world without the ultimate authority of an objective God.

Her grandsons for now are roving through the adolescent ages of ambiguity, where everything, including God and all His fallout, is subject to question. One thing is for sure: They are far more open to the idea that maybe ideas are just that—something to believe in to make things better. But that is an age-old privilege of being young, questioning all authority, believing in nothing too rooted, and indulging in an all too theoretical but none too practical world of flimsy morality and flexible rules.

Hopefully, at this point Wal-Mart Gus would pack away his gun, because ideally, as the world once again stitched itself back into civilization, fear would dissipate and control would be restored. This was merely the exercise that we all go through from time to time, right? A big, bad uncontrollable natural disaster comes our way, some flee to other lands, some to their beliefs. Some start questioning, and others simply retreat, armed to weather the storm. Is it so easy to go back when you've been to the other side, when you've witnessed what disorder looks like from the inside?

Perhaps you could restore the scenery, I thought. Perhaps, with the influx of money, the restitution of property, and the omnipotence of faith, you could make everything all right again, cover up the questioning and the fear and retreat to a life of choreographed sets, as we manage to do for television. Or maybe you couldn't. Shit, maybe you couldn't. Maybe whatever fear necessitated Gus to pull out a gun, Grandma Hill to invoke Genesis 6:7, Kel and A.J. to question, and my crew and I to paint a picture still lurked in the background—deeply rooted in the most intense, terrifying fear that beyond these facades is a world none of us can fully explain. What then? Can you go a whole lifetime patching the refuge together?

And if so, then is that whole life, this entire reality of one superficial moment patched to the next, an illusion, a matrix of fallacy, that covers up a deeper and fearsome longing for truth? What if "it's not all good"? Are we ready to confront the truth? Are we ready to step through that door and leap from the refuge of our beliefs?

It's that ultimate step into uncertainty that poses the most base fear of all. Are we prepared to confront a world that doesn't fit so perfectly together and shield us from the unanswerable questions of life? Are we prepared to face a life where the only certainty is that uncertainty? Ultimately, if one is prepared to make that leap, it can come only with a supreme sense of trust, not in a foreign scriptural God, but in a deep, empowered sense of self and the world we all exist in.

Several months after we completed our series on heroin, I was cleaning the files on my computer. Going through the log of e-mail addresses compiled in my in-box, I saw a note from my old anonymous friend from several months ago. I opened up the note, hit reply, and crafted a short note: *Remember me? . . .*

How are you doing? . . . I hit send and carried on with the rest of my day.

Weeks passed without any reply. In all honesty, once again I had forgotten about getting a response.

And then, in the middle of a mundane workday, swimming through the mysterious abyss that is the Internet came a note. I opened it, and it read:

Today I bought a new car. It was pretty cheap—really beat-up and old—but with a good engine that I can make run. I'm really proud because I bought it with the money I've saved up the last few months— money that I would have spent buying heroin if I hadn't changed. I thought I'd let you know.

By the way, I think I saw you at the grocery store. Also on the street corner and the other day at the gym. Were you at that Japanese restaurant just the other day? Because I think I saw you there, too.

We may be invisible to one another, but we know we're there . . . and that's nice.

Thank you.

Translators

Prince Siddhartha was twenty-nine years old when he left his life as heir to the royal throne. One night he slipped quietly into the room where his young wife and son were asleep, kissed them both, and then turned his back on the life that he had always known. He traded his royal robes for the simple orange one that the local sages and streetwalkers wore. He shaved his head, carried a staff in one hand and in the other a bowl to beg for money and fill with whatever food each day would bring. He put one foot before the next, not sure where the path might lead him, closing one door on the known and opening another on the mystery of uncertainty.

Surrender

Don Luis could be ninety years old. No one really knows. He guesses that he isn't, because he thinks that ninety-year-olds shouldn't be alive, that that is way too old to be loitering around in life. Luis, his son, estimates that his father is pushing ninety based on the fact that his father has been living in the hut twenty paces from his own for about twenty years. When I ask him how he knows that his father has been living in the hut for twenty years, he looks over at his grandson, who to my eyes looks about twelve years old, and says that the boy was born about the same time that his father moved into the new hut. Prior to that, his father lived in another hut, since destroyed so that the townspeople didn't have to walk through it to get to the town well.

I nod my head and try to figure this out in my mind. Besides the fact that Jesus—Luis's grandson and Don Luis's great-grandson—cannot be twenty years old, Luis's logic still doesn't make sense. Just because Don Luis may have lived for twenty years in that hut doesn't explain the prior seventy and how that guesstimate exists. When I ask about this, Luis smiles, points to his wife, who looks no more than fifty years old, and says that they have been married fifty years this summer and that Don Luis danced like a forty-year-old at their wedding.

Danced like a forty-year-old?

What does that mean?

I nod my head and pretend to be satisfied with these answers. The grin on Luis's face has been there the whole time, but the scowl on his father's face seems to be growing.

When Luis asks him in the Mayan language why he appears upset, he answers that he's now feeling old thinking about all of this. He shakes his head and leaves the hut.

I start to apologize, but Luis shakes his head and declares in broken English, "Don't worry you, fifty year, my whole life, he upset about something or other."

In southern Mexico, mostly in the Yucatán peninsula but stretching down into the central highlands of Belize, Honduras, and adjacent Guatemala, there are numerous ancient Mayan ruins. Tourists flock to these sites because, for the Western world, they are one of the most mesmerizing remnants of ancient civilization in our hemisphere. The written records of the ancient Maya as a people go back to around 50 B.C., though their culture is thought to go back much further. Over the course of almost two millennia, they managed to construct a civilization that reached levels of sophistication that rival the more heralded Egyptians and Greeks. When much of Europe was buried in the Dark Ages, the Maya culture achieved astonishing heights in the sciences and architecture and created a sophisticated calendrical system, all of which have astounded modern scholars who are hungry for more information on this once grand culture.

My crew and I went south in the winter of 1998 to do a piece on the Maya and their achievements. At present we were still at Chichén Itzá—perhaps the best restored of the Maya ruins. We planned to spend a few days there, followed by brief stopovers at other ruins in the Yucatán and then venture still farther south to Honduras and the ruins of Copán, a city that was still being carefully uncovered by archaeologists.

Perhaps what equally fascinates scholars is the way in which many of the Maya cities appear to have been abandoned literally overnight. Evidence indicates that the populations of these huge cities vanished almost without trace and without leaving any reason why. It's the type of cultural story that awes anthropologists and thrills theorists. There are few records left from the ancient Maya since Spanish conquistadors, in an effort to convert the "pagan" worshipers, burned most of their books. Today, only their ghosts lurk in refurbished tourist sites like Chichén Itzá, in the ball courts where ritual decapitations took place, atop the warriors' temple or at altars where the heads were shown off, and at the top of the central pyramids—where again scholars seem not to know what exactly occurred.

One complex trace the Maya have left behind are small villages like San Felipe, where Don Luis and three generations of his family all share two aged huts. People like Don Luis are relics in an eccentric landscape—they speak the ancient Maya language along with broken Spanish and even more broken English. They sit around doing mostly nothing—no working, no reading, hardly even talking to one another, while the generations after them watch *Baywatch* and the NBA (electricity and television arrived in San Felipe about eight months before).

If they know anything about the ancient past of their ancestors, they keep it to themselves. It's next to impossible to pry any information out of them.

Eventually, Don Luis returns from wherever it was that he had wandered off to. By this time, a small group of us have assembled a few plastic lawn chairs in the interior of the bare hut. We're traveling with a rather large crew this time—me; my producer, John; and a camera crew consisting of a shooter and soundman, both of whom have ventured outside the hut to shoot some local color. We also have some local guides along with us, a Mexican anthropologist named Rach and his kid brother—a local tennis pro and notorious partyer who serves as our driver/color commentator. The five of us are sitting in the shade of the hut, with Luis cooling off from the outside heat. Don Luis's scowl has shrunk to something more manageable as he takes a seat in the last remaining open chair.

Luis rises from his chair this time and exits the hut. Small conversations begin to break out among those of us remaining inside—Rach and John talk with Don Luis, and I turn to Ricardo, Rach's younger brother.

I ask Ricardo what, if anything, the ruins that we had visited mean to him.

"They are quite fascinating," he responds idly.

Why?

"You saw them," he says without expanding.

Sure. But I want to know if he feels anything more visceral than some fascination at a few old stones. I want to know if he feels any sort of connection to the ancient Maya, if he feels proud of what is obviously a very regal past.

Ricardo looks at me incredulously. The two of us have created a rapport the past few days, mostly late at night at the bar, where he, myself, and the soundman trade stories. We are three twentysomethings who find the most in common when we trade stories about our likes in music, movies, or women. But now he almost looks offended by my inquiries.

"Wouldn't it make for cute television if I told you how proud these ruins make me? That this is my ancestral past, and all its royalty, its regalness, somehow tugs on my soul and propels me to be something greater?" Ricardo's expression is incredulous.

"Or maybe it would be better television if I told you I could give a rat's ass, that these broken stones, these mud huts, are backward and primitive. That I could care less about some people who came and went a thousand years ago, that all I do care about is going to the discos, finding a girl, and partying. Which would you rather believe? Which would be easier to sell?"

His declarations have not come from a place of anger, only from a place of ambiguity. Should he relinquish the notion of an idealized past in exchange for the portrait of an uncertain future? I understand, because that's simply the way it is for most modern twentysomethings, caught between the globalism of the future and the romance of the past.

"If you ask me," Don Luis says through a translator, "family and heritage are a big waste of time. To hold on to the past is a burden."

But the past in this case, I declare, is full of glory, of wisdom, of exceedingly impressive grandiosity. The Maya, though less studied than other civilizations of the same era, reflect a sophistication that demands awe.

Don Luis shakes his head and scowls. His frown is so much a part of him that even when he agrees with you he grimaces and shakes his head vigorously.

"*Sí, sí . . . pero . . . ,*" he starts.

"Yes, but this is a culture that had many things—big buildings, great religion and culture, sciences, and other things," Rach translates. "Human sacrifice, needless war, ritual rape, great, great violence. To report just romantic notions of these things is too simple, too dishonest."

Don Luis and I, via my splintered Spanish, his broken English, and Rach's translated Maya, carry on a lengthy conversation about just how much of the Maya culture has been lost. Don Luis has a hard time estimating, he says, because he rarely thinks about things like this and, as I've learned, has a unique conception of calculation. "Customs, belief, religion— the things that make up a culture, these are not static things. These are things that change and transform constantly from one day to the next, from a parent's life to that of his children." He pauses briefly.

"That which doesn't exist cannot be lost. All things come and go," he says. "People come and go. Why do we attach ourselves to these things and force ourselves to feel sad when things pass?" He shakes his head, clearly not understanding this sensibility.

I understand his point a little bit but find that I am still stuck on mine—things like language and ritual are indeed lost from one generation to the next, but when they pass, it seems to me, something valuable is indeed lost.

Forced by my inquiries to contemplate earlier times, Don Luis begins to recall that many years ago the boys did not wear jewelry. They didn't rush home from school to watch television because there was no such thing. They didn't obsess about leaving San Felipe because San Felipe was all there was. Don Luis nods as these facts pass through his head. Quite clearly, he *hasn't* thought about these things before. At least he has not analyzed them to try to find their meaning.

Will these trends he's noticed in the young village people have some sort of effect on the future? If the young kids are being exposed to a world they didn't know before, isn't it natural for them to be curious about it and one day to want to grab on to it and in turn leave San Felipe?

Don Luis is an exceptionally bright man, and though he may not have thought of this before, the logic suits him fine and he nods. I wait, though, as my intention is to draw some emotion—does it sadden him in any way that he is watching his own culture fade in front of his own eyes with the help of an alien amalgamation of American culture? This is clearly perplexing to Don Luis. He cannot understand my seeming fear of things being lost—something so esoteric as "culture" washing away into something so mysterious as the future.

The scowl deepens, brought on by confusion at this unfamiliar mentality I have brought with me.

After a pause, Don Luis rises and motions me toward the doorway. He ambles outside into the warm, moist air. *"Venga,"* he orders, and tells us that he must show us something.

"*Venga, venga,*" Don Luis keeps muttering without looking back. We've walked through most of the village, passing the dilapidated schoolhouse, thin-wired fences caging wildly squawking chickens, hungry mongrel dogs, and lonely-looking livestock. We've passed through an unruly *fútbol* game played by lanky young boys, by a group of old Latin men silently playing cards, and over the dispossessed bodies of two liquored-up men lying by the side of the road. Don Luis doesn't take much notice of what's around him. He walks straight through the village without much fear that he is disrupting anything at all. This attitude serves him quite well—indeed, no one else seems to be bothered by him and his methodic strut.

Within ten minutes we've come to the outskirts of San Felipe—a lonely dirt road that leads to an equally narrow but smoothly paved road that is the national highway. Another twenty paces from here, Don Luis leads Rach and me off the road into some thick underbrush. He bends over, fishes through the bush, and digs out a long, rusted machete. The next beat he's swinging forcefully with it, making a path for us to push through.

The air in the central highlands of the Yucatán is always heavy with moisture. It smells fragrant and wet, and mosquitoes hover in flickering clouds beneath shady tree covers. Again Don Luis pays no notice. When he sees me fighting them off with wild motions of my arms, he chuckles. I ask via Rach why it is that the mosquitoes don't bite him, and Don Luis smiles.

He says that they just know not to bother him.

How do the mosquitoes just "know" not to bother Don Luis? What sorts of articles and agreements have the two parties agreed upon that prevent these little bloodsuckers from going after one solitary older villager? When I press for a bit more practical information, Don Luis becomes irritated by my questions. He comments that I am an analyzer rather than a watcher.

Taking offense, I note via Rach once again that I consider myself a rather astute watcher of things before me—that I am simply hungry for knowledge and understanding.

"There's a difference," Don Luis says, "between witnessing the world as it is and trying to force your own reason around it."

Don Luis talks without looking back, totally disinterested as to whether his comments please or offend. His sights are set on the path that he is carving in front of him. I, on the other hand, am fixated on his judgments of me, which means I am not too tuned in to where exactly we are—just another mound of swelled earth, surrounded by thick brush and crumbling stones.

I am soon informed, however, that this stack of dirt and stones is in fact another relic from the ancient past. Looking down the ridges that descend on both sides of us, one can detect an underlying structure. At the base of the hill is a flattened area covered thickly with vegetation that leads to yet another heap of earth ridging upward to another plateau like the one we are standing on. Even Rach, a seasoned anthropologist, is at first taken aback as he takes in the layout. After some inspection, and some inquiries targeted at Don Luis, he nods and reveals to me that we are atop one of the walls to the many ruins of ancient ball courts that spot the jungle.

I am thrilled by this discovery. Chopping through the thick vegetation of the Yucatán, coming upon uncharted ruins of ancient structures, I feel like Indiana Jones. Rach is hardly surprised. He notes that all throughout the Yucatán are many uncharted, and in some cases still undiscovered, ruins from the ancient Maya world. For a variety of reasons—from lack of funding to lack of interest—anthropological work in the region has slowed down significantly the past few years. Still, even for him, it is a thrill to come upon unearthed structures.

Don Luis stands silently at the peak of the hill, then lights a tightly wrapped brown indigenous cigarette. After a long slow drag, he speaks. "At my age, one doesn't measure life by what one has seen come and go, nor by what one expects in the future." He follows this philosophical pretext with a more specific declaration: "A thousand years ago, the people of Chichén Itzá and other Maya cities got up one day and left. Their reasons may have been many. What they left behind were large cities to grow old silently until the forest covered them and returned them to the earth.

"The same will someday happen with San Felipe—starting with these children." Most likely, he remarks, they will go to the "place in movies"—Los Estados Unidos—and he knows that most likely he will not see them again. He says this with a dispassion that is truly remarkable to me. A man who lives with four of his own generations, who has dwelled in the same village for his entire life, seemingly casually foresees a day in the not too distant future when the landscape of his life will change dramatically—when he will see his progeny simply walk away.

I know how this goes—or at least I think I do. We live in a world where indigenous cultures are indeed slowly disappearing—where we are all increasingly being defined by the same trademarks, dot.coms, and creeds ("Who wants to be a millionaire?"). We can write out this trend in countless eloquent ways because we see it in front of us—whether on a street corner in Toledo or in Tokyo. People like Don Luis are the last links to a different age, an age not so hardwired by the prospects of vision statements, business plans, and IPOs. They are watchers who are aware that they are being left behind. Why does it make me sad and not them?

I ask Don Luis again if it upsets him in the least—this idea that one day his own family will walk out on him. Sitting atop this mound of earth—this hidden swelling of heritage—Don Luis is more patient with my questions. The thin clouds of smoke from his tight cigarette smell like jasmine. It's quite pleasant, and it seems to have relaxed him—maybe me as well.

"You speak of the future as if it is something to like or dislike—as if you can hold it in your hands like a precious jewel—and decide whether or not you like it."

I remind him that he is the one who has predicted the future—foreseen the abandonment of San Felipe.

"A good likelihood," he agrees, nodding. There's a pause in our conversation as he ponders the notion of being left alone.

"Before one can be selfless, one must indeed be selfish," Don Luis announces. "But my children do not need to bear the weight of so many rocks." He motions to the jagged rocks and dirt all around us. "They do not need to live the lives prescribed by others, by rules and regulations held sacred because they come to us from eras past. The burden of cultural responsibility can be so great that a child will never escape from under its weight. These children live in a world that will be very different from the world of the ancient past. They must find new ways to deal with it. We would be foolish and selfish to hold them back just to indulge some ideas we have about the way things should be." He smiles and blows out another cloud of gray smoke. "It is no longer my time to be selfish—anymore."

The world around is indeed changing. And though Don Luis may not always understand, he sees the televisions and their images. He sees the boys wearing jewelry. He even mentions that his own young son—Luis—worships a God he doesn't really know, Jesus Christ. It is easy, he says, for a man to own many things in his life, from material possessions to immaterial ideas, but one must guard against those same things owning him. Because everything in life—from the structures that we are standing on, to the people who roamed them, to his own village people and the ideas that roam in their heads, they all come and go in the course of time.

He feels no sadness because he is not attached to any of them. His courage comes from confronting a world devoid of expectations. He is not at all intimidated by the uncertainty of the future. On the contrary, he is amused by the idea that ambiguity and improbability are things that could incur fear at all.

"In this world, you cannot be attached to anything—even that by which you call yourself. If you know yourself only by the titles that others have put on you—father, grandfather, chieftain—then indeed when they are taken away from you or not honored by someone else, you will become upset. But if you know that those things, those titles, like everything else in life arrives and passes, then you are not attached to them and you cannot be scarred by their disappearance."

The three of us stand atop the ridge of the ancient ball court. Ritual says that after ancient games played out there, the captain of one team and sometimes all the players on the entire team were beheaded. There is great debate among scholars as to whether it was the winning team that was collectively beheaded—awarded the honor of an accelerated trip to the heavens—or the losing team—penalized for their poor showing. Whatever the case, the ghosts of many warriors lurk among these scattered rocks and overgrown brush, and in a place like this, somewhere off the side of a lonesome road, beneath the rustling of the trees, one senses that time is the ultimate witness overseeing the drama that it is itself scripting.

Moments pass in silence until Don Luis continues. "For every man, there is a place he must go to find himself. That journey may take him from his family—to foreign and strange places. He may end up a bit more lost than he was before. And that journey may include choices that seem bad or wrong. But without going on that journey, everything in his life—his family, his culture—they all become obstacles that make his life more difficult."

I am not sure if Don Luis is talking about the life journey he knows his great-grandchildren someday soon will venture on, the one he has been on, or the one that has brought me here to him.

But he leaves that analysis to me—the analyzer—and offers these final words.

"Surrender is not only on the side of those who walk away from those things or people they are attached to, surrender is also on the side of those who are not bound by the actions of others, who are not the victims of what the world and others do."

To me, people like Don Luis exist on the other side of reality. They are like wizards who have the great platform of some strange life to stand on and stare out at the world with an enlightened perspective. Because so many revelatory moments have been strung together, they operate from a place that is itself a reminder of the strange incongruity of modern life: the images Pamela Lee Anderson bobbing in a Central American mud hut. They teach us lessons: *Surrender is the key to emotional freedom.*

The rest of us, perhaps in moments of fleeting reflection,

also witness moments of life's unconventionalism, where the odd imbalance of reality reminds us that there is no consistent standard the world goes by. Inevitably, however, we wander back to the monotony of daily living and stitch ourselves back into the matrix of a life without too much deviation. So the challenge then becomes in using the intermittent moments of revelation and the explanations provided by the likes of Don Luis as reminders of the crucial chaos that exists beyond the walls of "certainty" we build around ourselves. Those breakthrough moments expose us to a world of freedom that we all deserve. And it's often that we get these first tastes of real freedom when we are not restricted by our emotional ties to people, places, and/or things.

Real freedom, of course, is not easily gained. Real freedom comes only when we are willing to step away from the known into the swirling uncertainty of the world as it really exists. Leaving Honduras after almost two weeks spent in the jungles uncovering ancient rocks, I was relieved to be going home. Then it occurred to me to question what exactly home meant—a jumble of emotional attachments to family, friends, and, dare I say, materialistic items like my car, my bed, specific restaurants that I longed to return to after every long journey? What would Don Luis say? I wondered. Would he prescribe that the only way to find real freedom was to walk away from those things, leave them behind and face the uncertainty of a life stripped of everything familiar? Honestly, I knew I wasn't prepared to do it, yet I suspected that that might be the right path toward real freedom.

Sitting in seat 34C aboard a Continental jet headed for Houston, I tried to distract myself by picking up the airline magazine.

Just then, a middle-aged man came down the aisle and

stopped just short of me. He glanced from his ticket to the seat by the window, then agilely squeezed by. As he sat back, he sighed heavily and looked over at me.

"It's been a hell of week," he said, and shook his head. Reaching around, he struggled to pull his seat belt from beneath the seat cushion. "I have a feeling it's going to be a bumpy ride. It always is." He closed his eyes and sighed deeply once more.

I flipped a few more pages through the in-flight magazine and settled on an open page just as my new friend opened his eyes again.

He glanced down at the magazine. It was open to a full-size ad displaying a wide golfing green amid a palatial course with some old Maya ruins in the hazy background.

"Wouldn't mind being there." He raised his eyebrows.

I looked down at the ad. It was for an on-line investment firm. A caption splayed in thick white lettering ran across the picture:

It's not that far. Wisdom + Discipline = Freedom. This is where you want to be.

Don Luis might even be impressed.

Junction with Freedom

*Siddhartha was convinced that in order for one to become en-
lightened, to liberate oneself from the cycle of suffering, one
needed to rid oneself of all material attachments—had to
purify both mind and body of all desires. Having traveled
across the land, he came upon a small village on the edge of the
river. There Siddhartha found a quiet place in a clearing beneath a tree and determined that he would practice deep
meditation—observing but not attaching his mind to daily
thoughts that wandered the way of desire—and also undertake
an absolute fast. The journey inward, he reasoned—difficult as
it might be—would become his compass and determine the direction for the remainder of a life of eventual deliverance.*

Discipline

It's been three hours since our arrival in the Caucuses, a region
made up of southwest Russia, Armenia, Azerbaijan, and Georgia and mired in centuries of ethnic, cultural, and geopolitical

war. In the spring of 2000, my reporting adventure took me off to cover the war in Chechnya, a southern republic of Russia that has been fighting for its independence for hundreds of years, but most notably in two major wars in the last decade. In January of 2000, Russia had finally, for the most part, been able to squash rebellion in the state of Chechnya, killing and rounding up thousands of determined Chechen rebels who in earlier months had devastated Russian forces and taken control of cities all over Chechnya, including the capital city of Grozny. At the time of our visit, despite the Russian army's heavy presence in all surrounding regions, sporadic battles were still taking place in remote parts of the republic, along with common sniper killings and frequent kidnappings of journalists.

The Chechen subjugation didn't come without massive expense—the city of Grozny was destroyed. Less than 2 percent of the structures were left standing, the only modern comparisons being Berlin in 1943 after the Allies' heavy bombing and the remains of Hiroshima after the detonation of the atom bomb. Untold numbers of people—Russian soldiers as well as Chechen fighters and civilians—lost their lives in the conflict. Hundreds of thousands who didn't were forced to flee their homes for neighboring provinces.

I and my crew of three journalists, along with a Russian fixer (or local assistant) we had picked up in Moscow, likewise found ourselves in one of those neighboring provinces—a small village called Mozdok on the border of Chechnya. We had managed to stay with a local family, and as was custom, they had almost immediately demanded that we accept their hospitality by sharing a bottle of Russia's rainwater, vodka.

Eight of us sit around the table, the four of us, our two hosts—a young couple—and two of their friends from the village. It's late, though as in Las Vegas, clocks are conspicuously absent ("Time doesn't exist here," our host later explains, "only war"). The vodka is flowing, and our new Russian friends all have cigarettes burning in various stages. The air is thick with a choking smoke and loud conversations in multiple languages. Dima, our host, stands and hoists another shot of vodka in the air. He likes to perform like this. So far we've toasted to Jesus, Mother Mary, strangers like us, hosts like them, and countless other ideas that seem both ridiculous and profound.

This time Dima starts by announcing that we'll not find a more proud Russian citizen anywhere on the continent. He says this with gusto—a characteristic that befits him well. He repeats it. Then he is silent. The four local Russians drop their heads and there's a pressing silence around the table, so much so that I can hear heavy breathing from Dima himself. Then a toast is made to all of those who have died in this war—all those soldiers and citizens on both sides who lived their lives by the rules and ended up victims of a war that just won't end.

Endings are hard to come by, but beginnings are easy to identify because every moment is a conceivable starting point for another journey. Theoretically we have the opportunity to start on a new path every day—every moment—shedding whatever has bound us before.

For me the memories of yesterday, our first day in Mozdok, are drowned in several bottles of vodka. The following morning, my system demands that no matter what the danger, I need water. So I slip out the front door, slide by the rabid dog, which barks vociferously once or twice and then settles back down onto the dusty driveway, and head out onto the road in search of a local corner store.

Not far down the road, a young girl is walking with a heavily packed knapsack strapped to her back. She's bundled in a big jacket, thick mittens cover her hands, and a gray scarf wraps around her neck. But all these burly items cannot hide the skip in her step or the smile on her face. It strikes me as rather curious that such a happy young girl can even exist in this place.

She approaches me. "Welcome!"

She's headed to school, she says. Her name is Anya.

It's odd to me that schools are still in operation in this desolate army town on the edge of a civil war. In fact, I'm quite sure I've been told that the schools were long ago shut in this part of the world.

I inquire about this.

"My school is in my bag." Anya motions to the heavy bag slung over her shoulders. "One day the war will be over. It will only be our history, and we must be prepared for the future. So every day I take my books to a safe place and study."

It is the height of optimism to see an end to war such as the one raging in her world, but then again Anya has a clear and practical point.

One day—whenever it is—the present will indeed be the past. And no matter how much we try to plan the future, try to impose structure over future moments, the reliability of improbability mandates uncertainty. And though we cannot plan the future, we can prepare for it. In turn, it is the present that is the only thing certain. This moment, right here, right before us, is the junction of eternity, when past and future collide and produce the now. It's in the now that we are obligated and required to exist.

Even in the midst of massive confusion, the horrors of war, Anya had the wisdom to see that. Not knowing how long I'd be stuck in this forsaken place, I felt comforted simply by the presence of Anya.

She smiled at me and continued on to her school.

Rewind.

The first leg of our journey down to Chechnya required our flying via military transport. In the past few months, the Russian military had been flying countless transport planes down to the Russian Caucuses, carrying supplies and soldiers and often squeezing in the extra nooks and crannies crazy journalists whose primary goal was to get shot at without actually getting shot.

But as I soon learned was the general case in Russia, nothing worked on a precise schedule. Though we awoke at five A.M. to get to the military airfield outside of Moscow by seven, five and a half hours later we still had absolutely no idea when we'd actually leave.

Most of the journalists had retired by now to a shabby bar/lounge inside the officers compound. Though it was technically spring, the air outside was dry and biting and better left to stumbling-drunk Russian soldiers, not in short supply, who had been drinking vodka steadily since our arrival (perhaps before). Inside the bar, over a buffet of cold pasta and semiraw hot dogs, it was now the journalists' turn to trade quick swigs of two-dollar vodka. Most of the Americans and Europeans, myself included, refrained from the ritual, probably intimidated by the time of day—it was barely two P.M. But the crew of Russian journalists seemed at home with the circumstances and one after another came up with reasons to throw down more and more. Soon enough it became known that the reason for our delay was that our pilot—a gentleman who had pranced through the bar earlier and partaken of two vodka shots himself—had since disappeared. No pilot, no transport. Accordingly, the search for a new pilot was on.

Those on the bottle seemed not to mind. The rest of us, forced to surrender to the inevitability of such uncertainty, sat back in our seats and began to chat with one another. I befriended three journalists huddled around a small table—Kyle from England, Ben from Israel, and Nadya, a young woman who claimed to have been from so many places that she insisted she was from no place at all. All Moscow-based, they knew this commute and the waiting routine all too well.

"This is bloody bollocks—I swear it's always like this," Kyle remarked while lighting up his third cigarette in seven minutes. He'd light them, smoke them nervously, and then put them out disgustedly halfway through.

Nadya stared at this disapprovingly—in her eyes wasting half a cigarette was a despicable thing. She was a photojournalist who hoped to get into Grozny, Chechnya's capital, and pursue a story about female snipers that had spread like wildfire through the journalist community over the past few days. "It'd really be a very fantastic thing—such a fantastic thing, female killers and all—if only we'd get the hell out of here."

Wise old Ben—the oldest of the group by at least twenty years—leaned back silently in his chair. As Kyle and Nadya became more and more animated by their conversation, exchanging excitement, frustration, and strategy—each determined to come away with a compelling story in the next few days—Ben leaned toward me and inquired if this was my first trip to Chechnya. I answered in the affirmative, and he smiled.

"Good. Keep your eyes open—the best stories are the ones right in front of you."

Six hours later, we finally manage to board a Russian military transport, a huge behemoth of a craft. At least 150 soldiers are packed into the plane with us—all seated on metal benches that line the opposite sides of the plane. A giant causeway leading down the center of the plane is stacked with bags and supplies, and a few soldiers are stacked on top. Lazily they recline and are asleep before the last of the cargo gets loaded on. Some of the soldiers have passed out—too much vodka. Those who haven't hit their limit are loud and boisterous—singing and yelling. Drunk and armed, they're a sight to see. Shortly after we board, two of them are requested to surrender their weapons—semiautomatics that they give up grudgingly.

As the plane lurches forward and begins to roll along the tarmac, all the Russian journalists collect a handful of film containers and fill them up with more vodka, readying themselves for one more toast on the ground—they'll drink more in the air. I look down the dimly lit interior of the plane, its belly filled with soldiers and journalists, all seemingly oblivious to the adventure we're about to undertake and the utterly strange scenery that surrounds us. My stomach is raw from nerves. Though I've never been on a plane like this, through my experience traveling with various armies around the world, I know that they, and consequently we, are always a target. And now I am enclosed in by far the biggest target I've ever been on. I struggle to find comfort and security—there are no seat belts, so instead I clutch my Harry Potter book, the edges already worn from four days in gangster-ridden Moscow.

I look around again.

Kyle is buried in a deep, hard slumber.

Nadya is fiercely reading her book, *Girl, Interrupted*.

Ben is scribbling away in a small notebook.

The plane rocks back sharply and then starts rolling forward with increasing speed—here we go.

Upon landing at another military air base just on the border of Chechnya, it is made quite clear to us that we are guests of the Russian government and that during these tense times, we must submit to the orders and directives of our hosts. As with most wars both sides are usually guilty of the same crimes. In this case the Russian army has as many scandals, if not more, associated with their soldiers as their Chechen counterparts. Recent accounts of brutality, stories of torture and human rights abuses committed on behalf of the Russian army in news outlets all over the world, has made our hosts tremendously wary of the material that journalists would be exposed to. Additionally, in recent months, several journalists have also been kidnapped by Chechen rebels hidden out all over the area—reportedly even in the village that would serve as our base for the next few days. After their disappearances would come ransom notes, grotesque videos of severe beatings and mutilations, and sometimes replays of actual killings. As if reports of atrocities committed by their own soldiers weren't enough, by bringing journalists into a war zone, which the Russian army was obligated to do, they were also responsible for any actions committed by the rebels. To make a long story short, the Russian army had learned the hard way that wars are fought not only on battlefields—and perhaps more important won not exclusively by soldiers—they are also fought in the hearts and minds of citizens all over the world, fed with information provided by journalists and their reports. The tide of public sentiment indeed can be the determining force. It's a common tale told during wartime, and this would be no different. Opposing sides in any war obviously have different takes on the conflict and will try their hardest for you to see it their way.

Once we are escorted safely to our place of residence, the military alert us that we will reconvene the following day and set out for Chechnya, where we will be exposed to the insurrection. At that time, they will inform us as to what is "safe" to see. Until then, they recommend we stay inside at night—though, as we had already seen, the village was crawling with armed soldiers—and especially stay off the lonely roads and dark dirt alleyways that were suitable covers for lurking rebels and kidnappers.

But locals and experienced journalists scoff at these claims. "Sure, once in a while there are the abductions and these killings." Dima, our host, nods and smiles. "But no more than in that place you come from—Los Angeles."

By the time Dima got to toasting the many people who had died in this war, we had moved through a range of moods—playful joviality, irreverent humor, and now silent solemnity. Clearly, no matter how much vodka found its way through our cups, the reality of a battlefield outside the front door was impossible to ignore. Almost every family in the neighborhood, the whole village—in fact all the surrounding villages and provinces—had been affected by the war. From losing family members to stray bullets, to losing young boys enlisted in the Russian army or who had disappeared into the ranks of the rebel forces, Dima confessed that the war, even when the guns were silent, was quietly and hauntingly lurking everywhere around us.

I soon retreated to the living room—a small modest space made up of a stained leather couch and some spotty chairs. Mozart played from decrepit speakers in the corners. Dima made his way into the room as well and flopped down beside me. Small conversations had broken out all over the room, and Dima quickly struck up one with me.

"Why is it that you care about this war?" he asked in his broken English.

I gave him the standard reply about a news organization's obligation to supply viewers with information about what's going on in the world. He was too sharp, however, to be satisfied with this and shook his head.

"But you come now and they [the Russian army] show you nothing. They call themselves liberators and all this, and that's all they show you. But nothing"—he looked up again at me— "nothing, especially here, is that clear."

Months ago, when the Chechens controlled most of the conflicted area, including the capital, a few journalists had come in and been on similar detail with the rebels. They had seen the war from the angry, committed, martyr-inclined perspective of young rebels fighting for freedom. Of course, they had failed to reveal the brutality of their primitive behavior— the torture, the rape—just as the Russians would. The truth, Dima said, shaking his head, wasn't even out there.

Where is it, then?

If the truth wasn't out there waiting for us to find it—even if it proved to be terribly difficult—what, then, was our purpose in being here? I'd rather be listening to Mozart in my living room than his.

Dima smiled. "We wander strange places looking for things that explain what we're seeing, not knowing that that explanation can come only from the inside."

Food for thought. I smile, nod, and determine that I'll digest and eventually solve it. In the meantime, Kyle from England has managed to show up on our doorstep. He urges us to join him down at a bar in the village where a number of the journalists have assembled. I look to Dima for approval, as if he is my new foster parent.

"No problem." He nods. "It's dangerous but okay. Not unlike life."

I remind him that he earlier said that his village was no more unsafe than Los Angeles—a city I frequently go out in late at night.

How dangerous exactly was it? We had already come this far without much trouble.

He smiles broadly—the biggest one yet. "Coming this far takes very much luck. That you have. From here on, now you must just have *balls of steel.*"

In a basement bar located down a dusty alleyway east of the city center, a group of journalists has crowded around a few flimsy plastic tables in bending plastic chairs. Flickering fluorescent bulbs wrapped in red waxed paper dimly illuminate the small room with an odd, uncomfortable haze.

No one seems to care about the ambience, though. They are more interested in cups full of cheap vodka and local beer brews. Conversation flows on all sorts of topics from local and global politics to the unknown ingredients in the chunks of meaty-looking food stacked in the center of the tables.

"How are you enjoying Mozdok?"

Ben is reclined in one of the white plastic chairs, smiling up at me.

"Pull up a chair."

I comply. He offers me some food, pushing forward the suspicious-looking morsels and smiling as I stare at it.

"So?"

I stammer for a moment, still staring at the food.

Ben laughs and says it's okay—expected, in fact—that I won't touch the food. What are my thoughts about our present location and condition?

Having been there only a few hours, I have just one initial thought—that this place is depressing but I'm reassured by the fact that I am to be there only for the weekend. I hope we'll achieve our goals—move toward the Chechen capital of Grozny, get our story—and be back in Moscow within seventy-two hours. With that point of view, I tell Ben, I am able to take it all in with a detached sense of comfort. It'll be like football practice or a piano lesson—interminable experiences when you're enduring them, but ones you're grateful for when you've finished. I am quite sure that it will be a unique experience and that a weekend will be quite enough to get that experience and happily, excitedly move on.

Smiling, Ben nods and warns me about the small chance of everything moving efficiently enough to have us complete all our tasks on schedule. I feel a surge of anxiety—the thought of spending more time in this village is alarming.

"What you must determine," Ben interrupts, "is what story ideas you've come to find and how those intentions will influence the story that you manage to take away."

Having worked in the field of journalism for only a few years, I am unsure exactly what Ben is saying. To me, what he says seems more pertinent to a self-help book than to our current situation. Ben senses my confusion and has just started to explain further when Nadya—the photojournalist with no allegiance—grabs a seat beside us.

Our exchange of greetings and short stories from the last few hours is followed by an awkward silence.

My mind is still stuck on Ben's words. While not wanting

to be impolite in excluding Nadya from our conversation, I struggle to find a way to return to my exchange with Ben.

"Nadya, me dear," Ben starts in a way that only an older man can, "what is it that you've come to shoot?"

She stares at him with a blank expression. This is ground we've covered before. After a pause, she reiterates what she had said earlier in the day. She is interested in shooting a story on female snipers who are rumored to have appeared recently in Grozny.

"And other than that? If plan A must push toward plan B?" Ben asks.

Another pause. A single young woman traveling the world, armed only with a camera and a lot of confidence, Nadya seems the determined type who rarely requires a plan B. But she catches on quickly. "Generally speaking," she starts in an accent that is as elusive as her nationality, "the best way to shoot a war is to shoot the faces of those involved in it. The soldiers, the rebels, the civilians—their faces are the ones that reveal the scars brandished by battles."

At first this seems like an unlikely declaration. The war in Chechnya is one administered by advanced weaponry, rolling tanks, and roving groups of heavily armed men from both sides. This war story, it seems to me, would be told by these images.

Nadya nods. "These *things*"—she refers to the images I have pictured—"they all have a subjective impact on people. Without people, the violence, the war, the things that it is fought over—they don't even exist. The war itself is just an event, something that plays like a movie out there." She motions to the outside world. "But without an audience to observe it, it has no meaning. You follow?"

I feel that I don't entirely follow all of this, and it must show through my expression.

"The war doesn't have any meaning until an individual can give it one. Until a mother loses her son, a wife loses her husband, a family sees their house burned down, then only can there be some meaning to what is going on. For me, that is the only way to tell the story—those images. Those faces that are telling the inward stories of people."

"You must understand"—Ben winces as he swallows a mouthful of dark bitter beer—"that each of us depending on our own inward journey will see the world and the war in our own way. We are just participants from a different place in this war.

"You'll see that everyone wants to show you something different, wants you to see the war from their place. The Russians will want you to see one thing, the Chechens another. But only you will know how what you're seeing actually makes you feel. And that, that is your story.

"Because everyone has their own story. They package it and carry it safely with them wherever they go. They bring it to the tables that they sit at with strangers they bump into here and there. Wars dramatize those stories. They make the inward journey seem that much more intense. But make no mistake, the stories of the soul are never so silent."

The scenery is such that there are indeed a number of stories that can be told. Here the standard reality is guns firing, buildings collapsing, refugees fleeing. But the other reality is a stranger one, an ambiguous and personal one that I haven't figured out— what is the story I am going to tell? Though we are scheduled to be here in the village only two days, our time here soon will double because of the Russian army's continual excuses and post-ponements. Our fifth night I find myself back at the bar, once again sharing cheap vodka with familiar strangers.

So I'm still not clear, Ben, on which comes first, the inner or the outer world?

Ben clears his throat for the purpose of enlightening me. But before he can, a thick, pink-skinned Russian soldier ambles in and falls in the empty seat beside Ben. He doesn't care in the least that he is unwelcome. He turns and stares at me through glassy blue eyes. Though big and burly, he has a baby face, the appearance of an immature frat boy who is even more harmless and helpless when full of booze.

"Me Roman," he stammers, pounding his chest with his fist like a caveman. He wears only a thin white undershirt, the sleeveless type that doesn't cover his burly arms. Around his reddened neck, his steel dog tags testify that his name is indeed Roman Putin. Over the course of the next half hour and an entire bottle of cold vodka unto himself, Roman informs us that he is a twenty-five-year-old tank gunner who has been serving in the Russian military for eight years. In the past few months he had seen quite a bit of action in the Caucuses.

He confesses with a wicked smile that as a tank gunner he loves to fire indiscriminately into villages when the Russian army rolls their tanks into suspected rebel strongholds. He takes great pride in killing "fags," as he calls all his Chechen adversaries. I am not sure how to react—whether to squirm uncomfortably in my seat or suppress that impulse and simply nod.

As I adjust my inner scope and my outward appearance, Roman's eyes glass over, as if he is near tears, and he begins to speak tenderly about his wife and two children, who are waiting for him in a Russian village to the east. But then, in an about-face worthy of any trained soldier, his face twists into an evil grin and he starts to tell stories about the Chechen villages where he feels compelled to "satisfy" himself with a local woman whether or not she likes it.

Struggling with how to react to these grotesque confessions, I stare at Ben. From time to time he nods, listening acutely to Roman's tales, but his expression is as indifferent and as emotionless as can be. For months we have heard reports of torture, filtration, rape, and outright brutality committed by Russian forces unchecked by their superiors. It is the story that all the journalists crave to tell but the one the Russian army is guarding most fiercely. Now, right here in front of us, is a real live Russian soldier confessing to all of the above, and I either simply don't want to believe him or can't, because small things he does, like tearing up while talking about his family or seeking my permission every time he retreats to the bathroom, make me doubt he is the horrible monster he himself paints a portrait of. I soon realize that Ben is watching me as closely as I am monitoring Roman.

"Perfect test case." He smiles at me during one of the intervals when I excuse Roman to the bathroom. "Which story do you want to believe? Which story does he want to believe?"

Before getting to the answers, Roman returns.

Not wanting to drink anymore, I convince him that I am Muslim and have violated edicts of religious law by drinking—now I shouldn't drink anymore. The notion that drinking vodka somehow violates any sacred code confuses him intensely. But this wonder soon gives way to a far larger one. Up until this point, he has never actually sat at a table with a Muslim (in fact he still hasn't, since I am "faking" it), only shot at them from the interior of his steel cage. He becomes fiercely curious.

What God do I believe in?

What does my heaven look like?

My hell?

In my religion, are men punished for their sins or rewarded for their purity?

He shows me the silver cross he wears around his neck and talks about the purity of the Virgin Mary, how he will do anything to defend it.

Toward the end of the night, he keeps gripping my shoulder and pulling me toward him, repeating, "Friends—you, me—American, Russian—Christian, Muslim—friends." Again the tears have returned and hang suspended in his eyes.

I am not sure what is the fantasy—the ugly, killing, raping monster made by too much war or the warm, friendly, curious kid craving affection. I'm not sure which story I believe in or, the more I think about it, which one Roman believes in.

Eventually Roman excuses himself once more to the bathroom and never makes it back. We find him later in the hallway, passed out. I try to wake him and tell him to go home, but when his eyes open, it is clear he has no idea who I am. I am just some passing stranger he has run into in the midst of a world gone mad.

For me, Roman has crystallized the madness of the war. I want my new teacher, Ben, to explain it all to me, and on the sixth day in Mozdok, I seek him out and find him sitting beside a war memorial in an abandoned park. The memorial is of a soldier's hand holding a grenade, the pin already pulled.

"I wish I knew," Ben answers when I ask him which character Roman really is—the villain or the good kid. "Probably a bit of both—with fantasies of just being one—the hero or the villain.

"The thing you have to learn is that even in a strange world, where you end up in interesting places, sharing interesting times, you must never lose track of yourself. Let everyone be a road sign that points you in a different direction, but always realize that the road leads inside.

"All I can tell you,"—Ben looks at me—"is be brave. Take walks by yourself. Meet strangers. Listen to their stories, but most important, listen to your own."

We never did make it as far as Grozny. The Russian military jerked us around for six days and then decided to take us into a Chechen village where we were allowed, while supervised, to talk with some of the village people. I found a group of young male students—the females rarely came out because of the frequent brutalizations they still suffered. While a heavily armed soldier listened in, I asked some of the locals what it was like to live under the gaze of the Russian "liberators." The boys smiled, eyeing the soldier mischievously, and remarked in hyperbolic terms how great it was to have Russian soldiers "guarding" them. The Russian soldier, satisfied with this charade, wandered away in search of a cigarette. Then one young man stepped forward. He wore a worn-out, faded Philadelphia 76ers sweatshirt.

"Here we are at a juncture with our future. Our future is freedom, so here we stand at the junction of freedom." He spoke the words of a proud revolutionary. "All they need to know, all they already know, is that we won't give up. Our insides won't let us, so each of us will end up dying one way or the other because we won't surrender. There is no temptation."

As if he could sense it, the soldier returned, and the young boy drew away. He smiled at the soldier and nodded to me. In a few moments, our Russian hosts let us know that our time was up and that we needed to get back on the bus. As I walked back to the bus, the young Chechen boy ran up to me and pulled me aside.

He grabbed my hand and placed something inside it. I opened my palm to reveal two small worn steel balls, like oversize ball bearings that weren't quite Chinese medicine balls.

"These are for good luck." He smiled. "They keep you safe."

I stammered and told him that I was leaving Chechnya and that I would be safe.

"No, they're not just for Chechnya. They're for everywhere, because there's always a chance you could get lost. That's the way it is with every story—everywhere. They'll keep you safe. Like Superman"—he grinned—"balls of steel."

A Russian soldier spotted us. He came over and looked at the two of us suspiciously. I stuffed the steel balls in my pocket, and he shooed the kid away.

Back aboard the bus, I fell into my chair and reached into my pocket. I pulled out the steel spheres and let them roll around in my hand. As I looked outside, the boys collected in a small group, watching us as the bus lurched forward. They smiled and nodded. One of them raised his hand and waved as we started to roll forward. "Don't forget us!" he yelled.

I won't.

The window was just barely cracked open, and I was not sure if he could hear me. But even at that moment I knew that I wasn't saying it so much for his sake as for my own. I wrapped my hands tightly around my new charms and promised myself I'd keep them with me on all future trips. In fact, in just a few days I was headed for another war-torn zone in Sri Lanka. Feeling courageous, strengthened by the lessons I had learned from Ben and Roman and Anya, and equipped by a new set of balls of steel, I hoped for the best.

Dispatch from the Front

After six years of practicing these harsh disciplines, Siddhartha's body had withered to the point where he was hardly more than a skeleton. His skin hung loosely around his bones. His muscles had all but disappeared, and the features of his face were sunken. During this time, a man from the neighboring village sent his three daughters to see Siddhartha. "Come with us," one of them offered. "We will feed you and heal you and bring life back into your form." Siddhartha looked at the young maiden. There was no denying her youth and fullness. The temptation was potent—if the choice was between pleasure and pain, surely it should be easy?

Temptation

Dear Mom,

You'll be happy to know that I've survived Chechnya, as I am now on a plane leaving Moscow. I'm not sure if you knew exactly where I was, as I tried to spare you the details so that you wouldn't worry. But as you are a mother, I suspect you knew all along where I was headed.

War is a strange place. I say "place" because now that I have been to a few war zones, though the scenery is different in each place, the conditions and surroundings seem remarkably similar wherever you are. Most of the guys—and they always seem to be young guys—aren't sure what it is they are fighting for. They have these notions in their heads; they're convinced of their noble purpose, and for that they are willing to die. I can't say that I particularly understand because I am quite confident that if I were in their position, I would not be willing or prepared to die.

You'll be relieved to know that we never got close to any actual fighting; we saw no guns fired, no missiles launched, and suffered no casualties. In a perverse way, this disappointed us. Still, I do feel as though I saw something from the inside. I picked up bits and pieces, and though I may not be able to articulate any cogent reason for the ritual of war, somehow I do feel clearer.

I must admit that I am pretty tired both physically and psychologically. It was a rough few days, and despite the fact that we weren't at ground zero, it remained tense almost the entire time. And now, as you know, I am headed off to another war zone in Sri Lanka. I don't know much about it except what I've picked up on the Internet. The interesting part about it is that no one seems to be covering it. As opposed to the conflict we just covered, the war in Sri Lanka seems to be taking place in a vacuum of public disinterest. It's unclear whether people simply don't care or they are simply unaware. It's a bit of which comes first—the chicken or the egg. The government has imposed a tight censorship on all of the media, so I don't know even what we will get, but as I've learned, perhaps the journey to get the story is more important than anything we eventually do, or don't, get.

Love,
Gotham
March 2000

On the way from Moscow to Colombo a young Russian woman, by pointing to her pregnant belly, convinced me that she required my window seat for comfort's sake. Begrudgingly I obliged, squeezing into the middle seat while staring down at her protruding belly to remind myself why I was willing to endure such suffering for the next seven hours.

Ten minutes into our ascent, she leaned forward, grabbed her purse, and started searching through it. After a moment she pulled out a pack of cigarettes (half-empty already), settled the pack on her round stomach, shook out a cigarette, lit it up, and proceeded to start puffing away happily. When she caught a glimpse of the shock and outrage on my face, she pushed the pack of cigarettes toward me and offered one.

Perhaps because I live in the United States, where the government has taken a very strong stand on educating the public on the incredible health hazards of smoking, I found it difficult to understand how a pregnant woman could act so recklessly. As I stared at her through the smoke that wafted into my face, she smiled guiltlessly. She seemed not to have any clue about the Surgeon General's warnings, long-term health hazards, or prenatal deformities. If ever there was an example of someone being rooted in the present moment, through her own lack of awareness, her ignorance, she was a picture portrait, puffing away.

For seven hours, every half an hour or so she'd light up another cigarette. When she had finished her pack, and the duty-free cart rolled on by, she purchased another one and started in on them. Unable to sleep, I watched her, thinking that because of a simple lack of education, she was affecting the life of her unborn child in profound ways. These are the inner workings of karma. Perhaps, if she knew of the profound health hazards to herself and her unborn child, if someone had simply educated her, maybe she'd have acted differently. Because of the language barrier, I wouldn't be that person. Instead, as the smoke floated through the cabin, the wheels of karma just kept on spinning.

"It's quite nice, no?" My driver inhaled a deep breath. "Go ahead, breathe. Smells quite nice, no? In Sri Lanka, we have the freshest air."

"Come, come, come, look here." He pointed out the opposite window at the water that was barely visible underneath the midnight sky. "See the water? Quite beautiful, no? In Sri Lanka, we have the most beautiful beaches."

We carried on like this the entire forty-minute cab ride from the Colombo airport to my hotel, my driver giving excited orders and I complying halfheartedly. It was difficult to see much of anything outside in the dark, but my driver was excited, energized by the roads that we were rushing through. He pointed to everything, the smells, the beaches, the temples, the shops, the vehicles, the stars, even the slums, and remarked on how they were the best in Sri Lanka. I tried hard to keep up through my fatigue, but, having endured the nineteen-hour journey from Moscow, I was weary from my travels. I didn't know much at all about Sri Lanka, this small tropical island off the southern tip of India where I would be spending the next two weeks. But what I did know, and my taxi driver conveniently left out—was "in Sri Lanka we have the best war."

That's because in the small, paradiselike island of Sri Lanka, for close to two decades, a violent war has raged in which over sixty-five thousand people have died. In that time, the conflict has gone through lulls and flare-ups highlighted by vast aerial and naval battles, city occupations, civilian massacres, and parades of suicide bombers. The war is between the Sri Lankan government forces and a rebel group known as the Liberation Tigers for Tamil Eelam, or LTTE. The LTTE is an elite fighting force, nervously referred to by the U.S. State Department before our departure as a "pack of bloodthirsty murderers," or more diplomatically as an "officially recognized terrorist group." Though small in number, comprising eight thousand members compared to the two-hundred-thousand-strong Sri Lankan army, the LTTE—or Tigers, as they are also known—have managed to hold their own.

Like many conflicts around the world, this one is split along ethnic lines. The minority Tamil population, a dark-skinned Hindu people, want independence from the controlling Sinhalese, the Buddhist, more economically elite majority population. Though vastly outnumbered, the Tigers have managed through their extreme tactics to take control of most of the land that constitutes the homeland they want. These extreme tactics allegedly include the use of child soldiers, called "baby brigades," a frequency of suicide bombers, the slaughtering of their own wounded soldiers—to avoid the trouble of caring for them—and the commitment of every Tiger member, should they be captured, to swallow the deadly cyanide capsule each wears around his neck.

Despite intermittent eruptions from the notorious suicide bombers—increasingly, young Tamil women strapped with

C-4s who detonate themselves in public places in the capital city of Colombo—a large portion of the rapidly growing nation manages to keep away from the battle fray, which remains largely isolated in the northern and eastern parts of the island.

Up until now, the government, through their own relentless fighting as well as a carefully imposed news censorship on the war, has managed to maintain this virtual dual reality. In the capital city of Colombo and the southern resort regions, foreigners frequent pristine beaches, five-star hotels, and lively casinos. In the east and south, broken roads cut jaggedly through abandoned farmlands, bombed-out and bullet-riddled buildings, and dusty villages. People on either side of the island have little, if any, imagery of what the other side looks like.

Our goal, of course, is to remove these barriers—physical as well as psychological—and see what story we could tell. But it was going to be a profound challenge because no foreign television news crew had ever managed to cross over into areas controlled by the rebel forces. CNN and the BBC had been struggling for months with the Ministry of Defense to gain clearance to even approach the Tigers. And since very few journalists had crossed over and back successfully, no one had any clear idea of who these rebels were—including us.

Although we had logged many hours on the phone with the Sri Lankan government and had had preciously little interaction with the Tigers, managing just one short crackling phone conversation with a Tiger official in London. When asked whether or not we could talk to someone representing the Tigers when we reached Sri Lanka, he had responded, "If you manage to cross—and it is a grave situation, so to do so is very dangerous—we will welcome you. But we cannot help you in crossing to the other side. Our boys will be shot if they try to help you. You may be shot as well. But if you manage, they will know that you are coming, and when you get there you will see what there is." There was a pause filled only with the thick crackle of the phone line.

"You will see all that there is for you to see."

Having spent close to a week wandering the lonely, dusty streets of a Chechen village, I found Colombo to be the equivalent of a modern-day metropolis. I'd succeeded in my lobbying efforts to hang out in the city for a few nights before heading off to the more forlorn areas in the eastern provinces, so on the second night I convinced my colleagues to head down the street to a casino I had read about in the hotel magazine.

Within the first half hour at the blackjack table, I was down a large wad of colorful bills. I was content, however, to see the local bills as nothing more than entertainment expenses and dared not convert the amount lost to U.S. dollars.

Soon, however, it became clear that tonight would not be my night. I'd had runs like this in Vegas that usually got me depressed and angry, but this time halfway around the world and playing with foreign money, I couldn't really get that discouraged.

Just after another lost hand, a dark-complexioned man looking to be in his mid-thirties sat in the seat beside me. "Are you the group of foreign journalists here to talk to the Tigers?"

Caught off guard, I was unsure how to respond.

"We heard the report on the radio. It was printed in the papers. They'll have seen it, too—you must be very careful." He smiled and took a sip from the glowing martini in his hand.

My mind raced. Who will have heard of it?

"On the other side, they'll have heard of you. And you must be careful with them."

My stomach started to churn. These references to "them" and "they" were unsettling.

Who are you?

He ignored my question. "Stay focused here. Find the story. Do not get distracted by the chaos and the fire that surrounds it."

He rose from his seat, smiled and nodded his head gently, then turned and walked away.

Suddenly I couldn't enjoy the casino anymore. On the way back to the hotel I considered the stranger's words. What was it I would be distracted by? What was the fire surrounding the story? Was it the rebels themselves—the infamous "they"—that had me spooked?

"Suicide bombers? Oh yes, they are quite common." Mr. Wickrematunge smiled. "It's as if they are coming off an assembly line. Like that"—he motioned with his hands in a winding cycle—"one after another."

Mr. Wickrematunge was the editor in chief of the Sri Lankan newspaper the *Sunday Leader*. Through a variety of karmic twists and turns, as I like to think, after a few days in the capital we had managed to hook up with a journalist from the paper, Roy Denish, who had agreed to help us reach the eastern provinces and a town called Batticaloa closer to the regions the Tigers control. Though the national newspapers are under censorship and entire paragraphs in their reports are often blacked out by government censors, the *Sunday Leader,* in our estimation, seemed to be the most aggressive in getting at the brutal "truth" of the war. In effect, that boldness came with a price. The people we spoke with at the paper alleged that they had suffered under government muscle—intimidation administered by officials, often physical, to tone down their outspoken opinions on the war.

"It's quite easy, I must tell you," Mr. W. (it's easier for everyone) said, smiling, "to just go with the flow. Just abide by the rules the censors put in place and go along with the misinformation they dole out. I mean, who needs the intimidation, the harassment, and all that? They've shot up my house, pulled me over on the side of the street, and beaten me with pipes.

"But to ignore the war is to perpetuate the unreality of what is going on here. And that will prolong the war. More people will die."

Roy interrupted. "Yes, the truth can be very dangerous, but the temptation to ignore the truth is far more dangerous—far, far more dangerous."

There was a silence in the dingy conference room.

It was a curious statement and one without clarity at the moment. Dangerous to me was suicide bombers with no regard for human life, including their own. Dangerous to me was crossing sniper fields with the chance of being picked off by a shooter with an itchy trigger finger. Dangerous to me was getting stuck in the wrong place at the wrong time and having a hurtling piece of shrapnel rip you in two. What could be more dangerous than that? The answer was not immediately forthcoming.

We were huddled over some newspapers and maps spread across the vinyl-covered table, and the notion of danger was most likely uppermost in everyone's minds. A terrible war was raging and here we were, discussing strategies for how to get into the heart of it. All access to the northern territories had recently been shut down, as the rebels had in the past few days launched a forceful offensive and shot down a military plane attempting to get out of the region. But the eastern province was still open. And though access there was limited, Roy was convinced that some assorted credentials, smooth talk, and several packs of cigarettes to bribe soldiers with would get us through.

"Just so you know, though," Mr. W. reminded us, "it's very dangerous. Quite risky."

There was that danger word again.

Risky, how? I inquired as if there were some more depth that we could reach.

"As in one hundred percent risky if you were to go to the north. But since you cannot, alas . . . fifty-fifty where you are going in the east." Mr. W. smiled.

Mitch brought the camera down from his shoulder and rested it wearily on the table. "Fifty-fifty, what?" He smiled equably.

Everyone started to laugh. Nervous laughter, I think. Mr. W. never answered the question.

The following morning we started out early. The trip itself to Batticaloa was less than two hundred miles, but the road was crowded and badly maintained, and it was critical for us to reach the eastern provinces before nightfall. During daylight hours, the government forces maintained control of the roads, using fortified roadblocks. At night, everything changed as the soldiers retreated within their roadblocks, using them instead as checkpoints to prohibit almost all cars from passing.

The reason? At night, control of the roads turned to the rebels. Quite regularly they exchanged small-arms fire with the government soldiers. And every so often they launched mortar attacks on the checkpoints during the night. Consequently, the government troops had little incentive to come out—especially to assist nosy journalists searching for a story that was simply their lives.

As we neared the area where the checkpoints would begin, Roy became increasingly agitated. Our dilapidated white van rattled and roared as it careened over the broken road. Every few minutes Roy would light up a short unfiltered cigarette, hold it out the window he had cracked open, and take a few puffs on it before hurling it to the ground. Lalith, a newspaper photographer who had joined us as well, reclined in the front passenger seat with a hat pulled over his eyes, dozing. The rest of us, Mitch, myself, and another young producer named Laura, stared outside at the setting sun, acutely aware of each minute that brought us closer to nightfall.

"You'll start to see 'the boys' in this area," Roy said without taking his eyes off the road in front of us. He turned toward our driver and spoke briskly in a vaguely familiar tongue. "Faster, brother."

"The boys" is one of the names the Tigers go by. Though they are mostly confined to the "uncleared areas" that their organization controls, quite regularly individuals or groups of them elude the government forces and cross over to the "cleared areas." Sometimes they come with specific tasks—to deliver information or items to members on the outside, to smuggle things back over to their own side, or to carry out assassinations on chosen targets. And sometimes they come simply for recreation.

As we rattled through a small village, Roy pointed toward a group of young men loitering on the corner. I stared at "the boys" as we passed. They stared at us in the van. It occurred to me that if we could identify the boys, surely the authorities could as well. Why, then, did these guys roam so freely?

"They're scared. If the soldiers come in here, to the areas the boys control, officially or unofficially, they'll be slaughtered. It's happened before," Roy answered.

But we passed through uneventfully and before long were back out on the empty roads.

"On the other side, in the 'uncleared areas,' they don't have things like televisions, phones, radios. If we manage to get across, you'll see there is very little. The people live very primitive lives with no exposure to the outside world.

"What they do know," Roy started again after a brief pause, "is what they are taught from a very young age. They're taught to hate, and that fuels their will to fight."

The van drove into silence. On either side of the road, fields stretched into shadowy lands that were hard to make out.

"And then, when they come out, come across to these areas, they bring the hate with them and it spreads like an infection."

In this case, the infection kills. The Tigers who emerge from the areas they control are indeed considered some of the most fearsome killers among militant groups all over the world. The fire that fuels them is a deep, intoxicating sense of commitment to their cause and distrust of a world they do not know. They creep across imaginary lines, and in doing so, they enter a world that is their enemy. With them they bring a great terror, and in response, the world on the other side reacts in the most natural way it knows how—it tries to strike back.

We were officially late. The sun had set. As we approached the first of several major government checkpoints, Roy ordered our driver to follow his instructions carefully.

"When you reach fifty feet from the checkpoint, flash your headlights and then leave them on low. Then stop the car and make no movement. Lalith will carry the papers."

As we closed in on the first government checkpoint, our driver diligently followed Roy's instructions. Lalith waited patiently for our driver to go through the requisite procedures and then pushed open his door, took a puff on one of the cigarettes that he too was now smoking regularly, and stepped out of the car, clutching the identification papers we had obtained from the Ministry of Defense back in Colombo. Essentially, the solitary piece of ragged paper listed our names as members of foreign media and gave us clearance to pass into the conflicted area of eastern Sri Lanka. As Lalith exited the car, he stuck his hands straight in the air, sidestepped into the headlights, and walked slowly toward the checkpoint. This, of course, was a sign of submission, alerting the soldiers on the other side of the barricades that we were friendly. Eventually Lalith's slow march took him into the darkness of the checkpoint, and all we could do was wait for him to return—hopefully with good news.

We waited in silence. Roy lit up another cigarette. It was difficult to see much of anything in the checkpoint. The soldiers had buried themselves deep behind bunkers, barricades, and barbed wire. After inhaling deeply on his cigarette, still looking ahead, Roy spoke. "If we hear a gunshot and Lalith doesn't come back, somebody else will have to try.

"Joke guys . . . joke. . . ." Roy smiled when the rest of us failed to laugh.

Eventually Lalith did come back and we made it past the checkpoint. But this was only the first of many such stops. Though we were less than ten miles from our destination, it would take us almost four hours to reach it. The roads between the checkpoints were lonely, unlit stretches that our driver rushed through as fast as he could. Late at night it was well known that the boys watched the roads and controlled passage. After we managed to pass another checkpoint, and the car slowly lurched forward to the open road, Roy announced one more important instruction.

"Okay"—he took a deep breath—"now everyone must duck."

The driver looked back at him nervously.

"Not you." Roy shook his head. "You, drive. Fast!"

And we were off. Apparently reports received by the soldiers in their checkpoints indicated the presence of Tigers in the specific areas we were passing. As we crouched down, our heads close to the dusty floorboards of the van, Roy's voice whispered through the cabin. "They won't just shoot at anything, of course. But if they get nervous, if they're not sure what's out there, the temptation is to pull the trigger."

So that was how we spent the next four hours, alternating between ducking down in the hot, musty air by the van's floorboards while we cruised through the empty fields and shooting straight upward outside the checkpoints so that the soldiers inside could see us.

Some of the soldiers were annoyed at our presence, others impressed by our bravado, and still more plain indifferent to our cause. At one loosely guarded spot, the soldiers sat around a dilapidated wooden table, playing a game of cards and sharing a bottle of whiskey. They inspected our letter with moderate interest for a few minutes before the sergeant uninterestedly waved us through. But he didn't bother to instruct any of the soldiers to roll back the barricade, and none of them were inclined to do it themselves. So Roy, Lalith, Mitch, and I spilled out of the van and began the process ourselves—moving huge rubber tires, rolling away thick tree trunks, and finally peeling back jagged barbed wire.

For all practical purposes, this should have been one of the most terrifying evenings of our lives. And everyone in the car seemed to deal with fear in a different way. Roy would duck calmly until we reached a checkpoint, where he'd ferociously choke down a few cigarettes. Laura managed to lull herself into a slight sleep while imagining the comforts of home. Mitchell, the heavy camera hoisted on his chest, ducked down but still managed to rattle off endless questions: How much farther? How much longer? How many more checkpoints?

As for me, it made me nervous to think of the larger context of my own willingness to do this, yet it kept my mind off the implicit danger in front of us. Lalith, our loyal and courageous friend, seemed the most at ease, curled and ducking in the front seat without making any noise. And our driver, unable to do much else, he just drove . . . fast. Not bad for the fifty dollars he'd eventually get paid.

A few hours later we managed to reach our destination, a rundown ragged roadside hotel called the Lakeview. And indeed it overlooked a lagoon, across which loomed the "uncleared" areas that the rebels "officially" controlled. Meanwhile, not fifty feet from the gates of our hotel was a heavily bunkered barricade containing a few government soldiers. But even the proprietor of the hotel made note of the fact that the "officially" named "cleared" and "uncleared" areas were only of linguistic formality. "No walks at night," he uttered while copying our names into his pad of paper.

Having spent close to ten hours bumping around in our tiny van, the last four of them blitzed with the intensity of jeopardizing our lives, I wanted only to go to sleep. In my second-floor room, the only available light shone from a solitary dim bulb that hung from a slowly spinning ceiling fan. The linoleum floor tiles curled upward to the heat-stained walls. In the center of the room, two narrow cots lay separated by a thin aisle. The bare beds were made of thin wooden boards topped by skinny, stained mattresses. The air was damp and hot, the bathroom too basic to describe.

Depressed by the prospect of sleeping in such conditions, I turned around and headed for the dinner table. Fearful of the food, I was determined to find whatever local brew was on hand at the rudimentary bar and down a bottle's worth of it. By ten o'clock, Roy, Lalith, Mitchell, and I had, in fact, downed two bottles' worth of some local Sri Lankan concoction that tasted like a mixture of whiskey and wine, as we sat and strategized as to how we were going to attempt to cross over into the rebel-controlled territory the following day.

"The forces here won't want us going across," Roy noted. "They don't want people to see the truth, to see for themselves what things look like."

"Why?" one of us inquired.

"The intent of censorship is fairly standard. By manipulating the appearance of something, you gain a greater control over the way people think. You then force them to think the way you need them to—to support your intentions. Here both sides do it.

"And here," Roy observed after a moment, "it's been going on for so long, the combination of the war and the censorship, reality is so lost, so hidden and ignored, that the temptation is simply to regress into the standard roles—the rebels are the villains, the government troops are the heroes, and the rest of us Sri Lankans, we're just watchers who occasionally check in but for the most part carry on and accept those roles."

I noted the word *temptation*. There seemed to me to be some strange irony packed within it. I asked why.

Lalith smiled when Roy translated my question. He started

to speak in his native tongue, Sinhalese—a lyrical language that sings softly when spoken. After he spoke for a while, Roy translated back to English.

"He says that it's easiest to think of it like a relationship. In the early stages you put forth very much effort. You really try to make the other person feel your attention. But as time goes by, temptations come up, distractions come, and it is easy to lose focus on the other person. When you lose focus, you regress into familiar roles and you play out the things that are most comfortable, most convenient and habitual." Lalith smiled a guilty smile as Roy finished translating.

"Understand?" Lalith intoned in his strong accent.

"At some point," Roy went on, "here in the war, everyone got distracted and regressed. Even in a war, it can be easier just to carry on with the fighting than address the roots of the hostility that provoked it. Ultimately, wouldn't you say that we're all just creatures of habit?"

It's a familiar phrase—creatures of habit—but how does it parse in this context, within this idea of temptation? I asked.

"We all form patterns, observe certain rituals every day, that monopolize our actions. You drink Coke, I drink Pepsi—"

Lalith interrupted in his thick accent with a wide, increasingly drunken smile. "You say 'tomayto,' I say 'tomahto.'"

Roy glanced at him awkwardly before continuing. "Every day our reality is shaped by these habitual patterns of behavior—waking up at the same time, having the same food, going to the same job, talking with the same people, eventually thinking the same thoughts day after day."

As I considered this, it struck me that the real irony here is that temptation doesn't come in the form of the unfamiliar—the forbidden fruit waiting for us to bite into its unknown pleasures. Instead, it comes in the form of that which we are all too used to, that which is easy because it is comfortable and routine.

The temptation to fall into the familiar starts with an individual. In many families it happens at a collective level, when family members regress into familiar roles—father as authoritarian, mother as caretaker, children as rebels—and breakdowns of communication and affection take place. And inevitably it occurs on social and global levels as well. Different ethnic groups or races of people face off against each other over regional and other tribal issues of identity and ownership, and the product is civil war, like that in Sri Lanka, Northern Ireland, Palestine, Kashmir, the Balkans, and countless other places around the world where the same epidemic of laziness plagues people and results in the perpetuation of conflict. Finally, at the level of global politics, the same posturing takes place. The fact is that sometimes it's easier to feel the security of a hostile relationship than confront the insecurity of an entirely new one.

Silence ensued as we all sipped our drinks.

"I'm drunk," Roy noted, carrying on. "But it's a good example. When you are drunk you see things differently. You break the routine and see the world through a different lens. But everything here in this country, the newspapers, the news on television, even the way people talk about the war, it's all orchestrated so that people are not forced to watch from a different perspective—so they can continue to see through the same sober lens and not admit the horrible truth—the horrible bloody truth."

There was sadness in Roy's voice. As a journalist, I suspected he felt a noose around his neck, ready to snap him backward should he move out of line too quickly. By being with us, he was taking a chance and he knew it. He was daring to expose

to the world an ugly, deadly war that in two decades has sur-
passed the casualty number of American soldiers in the entire
Vietnam War. He was daring to take us to a place that few eyes
had ever seen, that no camera had filmed. He was doing all this
under the gaze of a big brother that fed off the familiarity of
control. Like a good journalist, he was speaking and acting out.
But even then, the real tragedy for him was that his voice would
still be muzzled—not by the government, but by a public that
was unwilling to break out of the conditioned paradigm
through which it viewed the world.

The following morning we crammed into our van and headed
toward the final government checkpoint that sealed off the
entrance into rebel-controlled territory. As the sun climbed on
the horizon, the town came to life with pedestrians and bicy-
clists funneling through narrow channels carved out by the security forces. Even in their own town, the Tamil people—a vast
majority of whom have no affiliation with the LTTE—are
forced to carry special identification cards. The government
forces that spill out of their barricades as the sun comes up
every day have the authority to stop or confront anyone and ask
for an identification card . . . and they regularly do. Such is the
life of the citizens of the eastern provinces of Sri Lanka—they
are prisoners in their own homes.

In between negotiating the crowded city streets, we would
stop and ask for directions to make sure we were indeed
headed the right way. One Tamil gentleman we stopped beside
peered into our van and looked carefully at all of us. Recogniz-
ing Roy as the only Tamil among us, he uttered a few words to
him while still not taking his eyes off of us and then nodded and
shook his head ever so slightly.

"He wishes us good luck," Roy said, nodding. "And says we'll need it."

I looked out the rear window of our van. The man had disappeared into the crowds of people that now filled the narrow streets and even narrower alleyways. Though the people of "cleared" Batticaloa are Tamils themselves, even they are not wholly familiar with the rebel Tigers. Most of them, in fact, whisper the name of the group with the same fearful and hushed tone that non-Tamils do. Though the Tigers have an extensive and complex network that stretches all over the globe and includes a plethora of Web sites that chronicle their credos, charters, and self-aggrandized "kills," their face eludes the entire world. Rumors swirl about them—the boys and girls that make them up and the missions they carry out. The same week we were there—just a few days prior to our stay in Batticaloa—there had been several "hits" imposed by the "pistol group"—a twosome of LTTE members who cross over from the "uncleared" area, carry out assassinations on specific targets, and quickly disappear. Though people have learned to identify "the boys"—we were told that members wore a specific type of pleated pants—they are never approached by outsiders. Though they pop up, intrude, and operate within the rest of the world immediately outside their walls, they don't mix. In and around Batticaloa, their faces are ubiquitous, their presence vaguely familiar, yet they remain strangers.

After a series of encounters at the final checkpoint that involved three hours' worth of smooth talk, arguments, telephone calls back to the Ministry of Defense in the capital, pleading, and manipulation, the guards finally lifted their gate and pointed with their weapons to the other side, allowing us to proceed.

"Good luck," one of the soldiers whispered through the

open window as we passed. He pointed to the camera with the long barrel of his gun. "Bring back pictures so we can see what it looks like."

That is indeed the unique irony of war fronts all over the world. Soldiers sit at checkpoints, authorizing entrance and exit from lands that are alien to them, whispering capricious fantasies to those who pass them by.

In this case, the irony of the "other side" is apparent as soon as you set foot in it. For the most part, it is made up of . . . nothing. Vast arid farmlands stretch into the distance, with only small thatched huts and narrow dirt roads to carve them into oddly manicured squares. Solitary cows, dogs, and donkeys wander here and there, grazing haplessly on the feeble remnants of greenery that spot the land. There are no cars, no working telephone lines, no pedestrians, and a total lack of activity.

Roy had more instructions for us to follow while driving through the rebel-controlled territory. We were instructed to sit straight up this time, so that anyone who might look in our van could see clearly who we were. Our driver had to tap his horn twice every two hundred feet to signal that we were friendly and in their land with good intentions. After driving through the lonely roads for almost thirty minutes, we wound our way to an LTTE office. There was one lone man there to greet us—a thin fellow with a light handshake and a severe limp. I scrutinized his pants and saw the three pleats—he was one of them, one of the boys. Smiling from ear to ear, nodding, rattling on in his native tongue, he ushered us to an empty room, where small wooden chairs were scattered across the concrete floor and a slow fan spun overhead. We all sat and he disappeared.

"What was he saying?" I asked Roy.

"He was apologizing that there wasn't a bigger reception for us. He's very nervous that we think well of them."

Irony again, I thought to myself. *He* was nervous. I was quite convinced that we were the ones supposed to be nervous. We were the ones sitting in the lions' den or, in this case, the Tigers' den.

All around us on the concrete walls were portraits—head shots of young soldiers, men and women, framed by garlands, beads, and other such ornaments. They were quite obviously memorials to many of the rebels killed in action. I got up from my seat and looked closely at some of them—the hard faces of the young people who had traded their lives for their cause.

In a few moments, our host returned, limping steadily, with a tray full of warm bottles of Coke. He apologized for the Cokes not being cold and gave us an embarrassed smile. He proceeded to tell Roy that the reason no one was around was that Tigers from the local unit had gone on a morning mission and were still not back. It seemed a rather ambiguous statement, and Mitch inquired what the morning mission entailed.

Roy translated the question, and again our host smiled bashfully and answered in Tamil.

"They attacked a military outpost this morning—killed eleven government soldiers." Roy paused and smiled at us. "They should be back soon."

After waiting for another hour, we slowly began to get bored and subsequently bold. Despite the protests of our host, everyone started to wander outside the steamy room, peering around the corners of the little office and walking down the dirt path that led from it. And then a solitary scooter emerged in the distance, kicking up dirt as it careened toward us. Anxiously everyone scurried back toward the office and waited to see who it was. One of the things Tigers are known for are the unmarked, often stolen, red Honda scooters that they travel on. As the guy got closer to us, it was easy to make him out— a young male Tiger with a rifle strapped to his back. He zoomed toward us, finally parking his bike right beside the office. After jumping off his bike, he pushed his gun farther down his back and reached a hand out to shake ours.

We spent ten minutes or so with this fellow, who had few details except to reiterate that the local unit had been involved in a skirmish early that morning. According to him, the government soldiers had sustained eleven casualties and their rebel unit had suffered none. Yet he also mentioned that they would not be returning to meet us—that they had got "caught up" on the way back and were very sorry for this inconvenience.

We had determined earlier that for safety reasons we would spend only the afternoon in rebel territory and cross back by dusk. No one wanted to get stuck between the two sides after dark. This meant time was precious. After huddling together for a moment, we determined that the best use of our time was to see as much as we could and then start back toward the other side. Our host nervously relented, despite the fact that he had no orders to do so. We all packed in the van and headed out.

The resulting drive with intermittent stops at memorials, farmhouses, and finally a Hindu temple, lasted a few hours. Our Tiger official very proudly displayed these places to us, mentioning at each one how many Tigers had died for it to be erected. The Hindu temple was erected at a site where nearly fifteen years ago a massacre of Tamil people had taken place. Over one hundred Tamils had died.

"For us"—our host nodded as Roy translated—"in this place, almost everything is because of death." A stunning and curt statement.

As we were walking back toward our van, Mitch noticed two young women dressed in dark green fatigues, huddled with a group of other onlookers inspecting us curiously as we passed. He asked Roy if it were possible for us to interview them. Roy, without looking to our host for permission, nodded— "quickly."

After jamming the microphone into the camera, I began asking questions as Mitch struggled to get the camera rolling. We blazed through a series of questions and answers in a few minutes.

The young women we were speaking to were teenage Tigers, seventeen and eighteen, respectively, both of whom had been serving for multiple years. As I spoke to them, they shied away from looking straight at me, looking bashfully at each other, each hoping the other would supply the answer. It soon became clear to me this wasn't because they were afraid of what they might say, but instead were simply shy, young teenage girls afraid of the camera. They shuffled nervously in place, answering my questions with one-word answers and nods. After a few minutes our host told us that was enough. I fired off one more question—What kind of fighting had they been involved in?—and got their answer.

"Front lines," one said through Roy.

"Killing," the other whispered coldly.

We shook hands and thanked them before stepping back. "Do you want to know how many they've killed?" Roy asked.

I wasn't sure I wanted to but nodded anyway.

"She's killed five soldiers—hand-to-hand combat." Roy referenced the seventeen-year-old with his hand and then pointed to the other older one. "She's killed one. Not too bad."

And with that we were off, back in our van, with no time to digest what we had just witnessed—two teenage girls who, were they on the other side of the world, might be lusting after some boy band instead of acting as deadly killers in a violent guerrilla war. After driving for a while, we stopped at the behest of our host and picked up a young man. He climbed into the back of the van and plopped down beside Laura and me. Like our host, he was dark-skinned with a wiry frame. As I shook his hand, I noticed something odd about his grip—not only was it soft, something I had become accustomed to in the East, where men shake Westerners' hands out of a sense of alien obligation, but it felt awkward. When I looked down at his arm, it was clear why. His arm was mangled, bent awkwardly at the elbow, with rough, rugged skin running over his disfigured hand. I tried not to react, but he'd already caught me staring.

Unaffected, he rolled up his sleeve and showed his crippled arm to Laura and me. It was horribly bent and the bone appeared only moderately there. He told us that a year ago he had been the victim of some sort of explosion. It wasn't clear whether it had come via a grenade, a shell, a launched rocket, or some other firefight. No longer able to be in combat, he was no longer considered a Tiger. He showed us the vial of cyanide he still wore around his neck and said that because he no longer had a purpose, he had considered taking it as recently as a few weeks ago. But in recent days he had been convinced there might be another life, that maybe beyond fighting there was something he could do. I asked him how he had come to this decision. He looked closely at our host, riding in the front seat, oblivious to the conversation we were having in the rear.

He started to speak softly, and Roy translated equally quietly.

"I started to wonder if my only use was to fight and to kill. For so long that's all I knew, it's the only habit I had—fight, kill. But when I was hurt, I no longer could fulfill my purpose, and all of a sudden the world looked different to me—it had no use for me."

He paused for a moment.

"But now I see differently, and maybe I do have another purpose. Maybe the familiar thing wasn't the best thing to do." He started to roll down the sleeve of his shirt and then smiled, referencing his disfigured limb. "And I have this to remind me of that every day."

Before long we reached our last stop, a village graveyard that contained six hundred graves, mounds of dirt lined up one next to the other that memorialized soldiers killed in action. As we wandered through the narrow lanes that separated the graves, I looked down at the scribbled placards that lay on two graves at my feet. The date read only a week ago.

Our friend with the crippled arm had taken to following Roy. He rattled on until finally Roy pulled his reporter's notebook from his pocket, scribbled something down, ripped off the page, and handed it to him.

What does he want?

"He wants a ride back to Colombo. That's where he thinks his new life is." Roy smiled and looked at me. "Just for a little while, before he goes to the States and makes his millions." I glanced over at him and he nodded forcefully, with a twinkle in his eyes.

"Don't worry," Roy said. "I gave him a fake name and a fake address on the other side. We can't give him a ride back—the soldiers would have our heads."

After about half an hour in the graveyard, a bell started to ring, signifying five o'clock in the afternoon. The time had come to begin our journey back, so we started to the Tiger office to drop off our two new friends before heading back for the other side. After about five minutes of silence inside the van, our host turned around in the front seat and stared at all of us in the back. He fiddled with his shirt and pulled out his cyanide capsule. Some dark thick liquid had settled at its bottom.

"This is the sign of our determination—we are willing to kill and be killed." Roy struggled to keep up with him, as all of a sudden, as if he had been saving up his words, they began spilling out fast and furious. "Killing is a hard business to be in. For killing can take a lot out of you. To take another life, even if it's with a gun from far away, without seeing it take place straight in front of your eyes—it's still very odd. So you have to put it aside, you have to or you can't go on knowing that every day another brother, another son, another father, is dying at your hands. But see, when you take that emotion out of it, when you no longer let those thoughts creep into your head, then it is impossible to break out of it. I kill because I have to, because that is what I know my duty to be. Nothing else. I will die also, I will . . . and I am not afraid."

For the rebels, killing and violence satisfies a primal need for achievement. In a life and land where nothing much is available, killing takes them somewhere. It provides them with a purpose. And because, like fundamentalist rebels the world over, they believe so forcefully in their purpose, their determination is deep, soul-felt, and its life is worth more than theirs. This is their faith. And it allows them to invest their energy, attention, and intention into something that supplies meaning to their life—no matter how thin and fragile it is to those of us watching from the outside.

While our host had been speaking, I had been watching our disfigured friend in the back of the van. He seemed to have turned the corner through his forced act of witnessing. Because he couldn't kill anymore, he was convinced that he had another purpose—maybe in America making millions. Perhaps if he had never been a half casualty of war, he might have remained in the familiar role that the other soldiers on both sides had. Instead he had been forced into a conscious act of witnessing, and in doing so, he may have found a new path—an unfamiliar one that might offer some sort of salvation.

But alas, the likelihood of his achieving freedom from the temptations of familiarity were slim.

The next morning we all were up bright and early, charged by the intensity of our achievement the prior day. Before we went, the hotel staff brought out some eggs, toast, and tea. As I came down from my room, I noticed an unfamiliar face sitting beside Roy at the breakfast table. As I sat down, Laura nudged me and made eyes directed toward the stranger's pants. I looked down—pleats. We were sharing breakfast with one of the boys.

I wish I could report that we shared a heartfelt conversation that delved into the nature of war and warriors. But we didn't. No one, it seemed, felt particularly inclined to penetrate those shady areas. In fact, the most astounding thing about the Tiger we dined with was that he didn't make much of an impression at all. He appeared to be a normal guy eating a normal breakfast caught in a crazy war fought in a crazy place.

And indeed, it is these seemingly innocuous people who are enmeshed in the wars the rest of us often push back in our awareness—either because of censorship or through simply ignoring them. In this way our efforts are complicit—they are willing to keep fighting no matter the toll, and we are willing to ignore the horrible truths of war. Among the several soldiers we met, only one—the young man who had had his arm crippled in battle—had gained a larger awareness of the world that had ensnared him. He was the only one whose loss of routine had gained him greater awareness. And that for me had proved to be perhaps the most terrifying thing—that the soldiers who fight in these wars are just like the rest of us. But instead of having been programmed and tempted by the fruit of the comfort and familiarity of a job or relationship, they have been programmed to kill.

Social ailments like these don't necessarily have remedies. The reason that indifference, apathy, and ignorance exist on personal and global levels is because it's so easy for us to forget and slip into the level of awareness where we want to be reminded only of what makes us comfortable. Sometimes there are added forces that make these ends unfortunately easier to reach.

Several months after our return from Sri Lanka, the *Sunday Leader* was shut down. We weren't terribly surprised. But further shocking news soon arrived. Roy had been picked up by government authorities, and it was being reported on the local government–controlled news agency that he was being accused of holding secret talks with some of the Tigers while posing as part of a television crew that had crossed over to talk with the LTTE. The television crew, of course, was ours, and the charges, of course, were false. The price, however, was steep. As in most countries around the world, treason equals death in Sri Lanka. Through his subsequent e-mails that were increasingly desperate and less and less detailed upon the goings-on halfway across the world, it was clear that Roy was in trouble. He had dared to tell a story, to confront the lies the government used to reinforce their false reality, and now he was paying the price for his courage.

Roy had taken us to the "other side" and back. The other side had promised intrigue, mystery, revelation, and adventure. And the journey had supplied all of those elements in uniquely ironic ways—for the other side was a physically naked, abandoned wasteland waiting in limbo for a two-decade-long war to resolve itself. But its barrenness had provided insight. Its unfamiliarity to the other side allowed its citizens to remain wedded to their belief system. The other side had delivered a guiding principle to those of us who had managed to cross over, survey it, and return: No matter the temptation of the familiar and comfortable, it is imperative for each of us to occasionally step into the vast expanse of the unknown. Only then can we be prepared to continue our journey forward.

God Willing and
Rock & Roll

*Though he had managed to stay the course and avoid falling
prey to temptation, Siddhartha knew he was no closer to enlightenment than he had been when he started his quest six
long years ago. In fact, he now saw his method had been
wrong. The road to enlightenment didn't involve closing oneself off, but rather opening one's awareness fully to the world
around him. The road to enlightenment was paved with neither debauchery and excess nor suffering and denial—it lay
smoothly along the middle. And most important—freedom
was not a place to arrive, but a state in which to travel. Freedom was not a state of obscure complexity, but one of astounding, life-altering simplicity.*

Enlightenment / Freedom

"We didn't have much use for these terms, you know: Hindus,
Muslims. You live there. I live there. We were kids, then, really
just kids. And neighbors."

I can tell from the way Prem uncle says this, with a tight frown on his face, his neck craned, and his old eyes gazing up toward the roof, that he means it . . . or at least he meant it.

"We were twenty-two, twenty-three years old, like you, no?" He shoots a glance at me, nods, and doesn't wait for confirmation. I'm twenty-five, quizzing him about events fifty years ago. Prem uncle doesn't care much for details anymore. Little details like labels, ethnicities, religions, they ruined his life fifty years ago, and since then they haven't much interested him.

"We went to the bars and the clubs and drank together, got drunk together—every Indian loved Scotch in those days—the town, all of Lahore, it was ours. It belonged to us."

In 1947, India had just gained independence from its colonial ruler, Great Britain. Like many colonial outposts, until that time civil tensions had taken a backseat to resistance against the more immediate problem of imperialist rule. But the unrest and brewing animosity between Hindus and Muslims that had existed in India for hundreds of years was again at the point of eruption.

"It was a very crazy time. All of a sudden 'freedom.' What did that mean? Things from yesterday hadn't changed at all, and yet everything, *everything,* was different.

"There were celebrations in the streets. People yelling, 'Freedom!' Really just shouting it as loud as they could, hoping it would teach them what it meant because no one knew. But then, the celebrations, they turned to riots."

There's a change in the tone of Prem uncle's voice. His eyes are downcast, perhaps still a bit perplexed. "Small disturbances, fights, and all of a sudden they became huge riots."

Indeed, throughout the independence movement in India, there had been factions urging for the separation of nations— the creation of two countries to serve as home for the subcontinent's two major faiths—Hinduism and Islam.

And so the state of Pakistan was born. Granted its independence in 1947, Pakistan secured official partition from India in August of 1948. Overnight, regions that for thousands of years had been a part of India's royal history had a new name, a new face, and an unknown future.

"We weren't sure what we were supposed to do, where we were supposed to go. How we were supposed to feel," Prem uncle recalls. "All of a sudden we were guests in our own home. It was very strange. How were we supposed to act? We didn't know.

"So we did what was most natural: we just carried on. We went to work."

But simply going to work proved life-threatening. Animosity fueled by weeks of national transformation spilled into violence. On both sides of the border, riots broke out each night. In Delhi, Muslims, residents of the city for hundreds of years, were slaughtered on their doorsteps. The same gruesome fate was met by thousands of Hindus who lived in Lahore.

"In the morning, going to work, we'd see corpses—just strewn along the side of the road. How had our city, our home, turned into a war zone?"

Determined not to surrender their homes to such anarchy, young men like Prem uncle insisted on going to work. But they did take certain precautions—like wearing Muslim clothing to conceal that they were Hindus.

"No one could tell," he says with the hint of a smile. "Our friends at the office knew, and we just laughed. It was a joke. Inside the buildings, no one cared which God we believed in. Out on the street, no one could tell the better. We all looked the same—*we all were the same*."

The same, but different. It's like a riddle of wording in a

Nabokov novel or in a play by Shakespeare. The dressing on top disguises similarities beneath.

"I think I knew the day that it was over." Prem uncle looks at me sadly. "I think I knew, but I didn't want to admit it.

"Indir, my brother-in-law, he was a police inspector, he came to the office that day and told me that his neighborhood had been attacked. All the Hindus were being attacked and he was going to leave—leave that day for the border and go to India.

"I wasn't sure what I was going to do. My neighborhood seemed safe. I was young, of course, and stubborn. I was going to leave my home? And go where? Just like that? No, I was going to stay, and I told Indir so.

"That was that. Indir nodded and said okay. He understood. He was married to my sister. I was still not married. I could afford to stay. He said they were leaving that night, that Bimla, my sister, had already gone to Delhi, and that he was returning to the house to pack some things and then they were going to leave—he, his mother, and his sister." It's clearly not a story that Prem uncle has often told before. There's a break in his voice every so often. It gets soft, and then he readjusts and strengthens his tone. Today he is well into his seventies. He's a small man, like his sister, my grandmother. Within the family, he's always been a favorite of the kids. Not because he's good with kids—he's not. He has none of his own and doesn't seem to have much affection for young children. Growing up, though, we recognized him as the patriarch of the family. He was the one the elders went to for help. All families have to deal with the dramas of things like substance abuse and adultery, and some have one unilateral authoritarian who cleans up the resulting messes. Prem uncle was ours—we even jokingly called him the "Don." He had no idea what we were talking about.

It was very rare that he appeared vulnerable, not because he felt a need to hide that side of him, but simply because he was a loner who never required the guiding hand of someone else. Researching our story on the war in Kashmir, the conflict between India and Pakistan, I had gone to him for some guidance, knowing only that he had grown up in the city of Lahore when it was still part of India. Sitting with my producer, Mitch, in a redecorated colonel's club at the top of the Taj hotel in downtown New Delhi, listening to my great-uncle's story, I felt privileged to think that he was revealing a side to me that few had seen.

"I told him not to go, just to leave, because things were very unpredictable and going back to the neighborhood where he knew there was trouble didn't sound like a good idea." Prem uncle gives a gentle laugh. "Though he was married, he was young and stubborn like me. And that police inspector's badge, I think it made him feel safe."

But Prem uncle sensed that it wasn't safe, that the riots were too familiar now to pretend there wasn't danger everywhere. Though he tried to convince his brother-in-law of his fears, he wouldn't listen.

"So I insisted I go with him. He was my sister's husband. It was my duty to look after him." There's not a sense of pride when he says this but, as he says, simply a sense of "duty."

"We climbed into the car—the four of us—Indir, me, his mother, and his sister. We drove to his town. It wasn't very far. When we did get close, you could see that there was trouble just in front of their house. So Indir parked the car down the road and told his mother and sister not to move.

"We went to the house, and just in front there were groups of young Muslim men shouting slogans and all that. They were a rather intimidating lot, all of them like that swaying together and chanting. Even Indir was scared, I think.

"We went into the house, and collected a few things, then decided to leave. The crowd outside was getting bigger and louder. When we got back to the car, all was fine and we were just going when Indir remembered one small item left in the house that he must not leave behind. Some item, I'm not even sure what it was." Prem uncle shakes his head.

"When we went back the second time, the crowd had gotten really big, When we came out from the house, boys were everywhere.

"Indir saw it first, a group of boys gathered around the car. They were pushing it and banging on the outside. Indir screamed at them and ordered them to stop. When they saw his uniform, they got even more mad. But Indir was equally angry, seeing how they had scared his mother and sister. He shouted something at them, and then they knew he was Hindu. He was Hindu and he was a police inspector, and that did it. All of a sudden there was fighting and more shouting and yelling, and a big group of them were all over him, beating him hard."

Silence.

"I tried to do something, but there was so much confusion and so many people that no one knew what I was doing. And no one knew I was Hindu—I had on the Muslim dress I wore to work. They thought I was one of them. So there I was, helpless, unable to do anything as they beat Indir up and dragged his mother and sister from the car and beat them, too. I watched them beat him to death, my own brother-in-law, whom I was supposed to protect."

Irony is a strange thing—it bends in so many ways. Prem uncle knows both sides of this equation—had he not been wearing that dress, most likely he too would have been beaten and perhaps killed. The young man in him also believes that had he been dressed differently, he might have been able to stop them. But it is futile to twist history in any other shape than it is.

Eventually police officers appeared on the scene. Seeing one of their own slain, the officers began to take retribution on all Muslims in the area. Besieged on all sides and caught in the confusion was Prem uncle—mistaken by the killers and now at the mercy of the officers.

"I just started to run, but one of the officers caught up to me. He recognized me as Indir's brother-in-law. He knew I was in danger, the way I was dressed. He grabbed me and put me in the back of his car. And then we just drove away, leaving everything behind. He drove me to my own car and told me to get out of Lahore, not to stay another hour. Just go to the airport and leave.

"So I did. I drove there in the clothes I was wearing without going home. I never saw my home again. I didn't retrieve a thing, just went to the airport, left my car, boarded the plane, and left. Just like that."

That same night, the riots in Lahore reached a climax. Half the city was torched. Hundreds of Hindus were slaughtered in the streets, and lines of partition and hostility were drawn between two countries that days before were one.

Prem uncle has told me most of his story now. Having opened the door, he once again seems to be closing it—the familiar scowl returns to his face. "We were friends and neighbors and then we were enemies—all in a few days, a few hours. If those men had known who I really was, maybe I could have stopped them—Indir would not have been alone or maybe they would have killed me as well. But because of the clothes, those robes I wore that day, everyone was confused. Maybe it was fate. . . ." Prem uncle pauses. It's not clear whether he believes in fate or is just an old man who's trying to believe his clichés.

"I watched them beat my brother-in-law to death and I couldn't do anything to stop them. And me, they were just confused when they saw me, they never saw the man beneath them. The clothes—they saved my life that day, but I think they robbed me of something else."

Is there literally a line somewhere where you can put one foot on one side, the Indian side, and place your other foot on the Pakistani side, and be in both places?

"Technically, no," Raman uncle answers me, not entirely clear whether my question is serious or not. "There are zones in between the two borders that are 'gray zones,' if you will. In the army, we consider them no-man's-lands, neither here nor there—they don't belong to anyone save the man who is crossing from one side to the other."

There is a silence as we sit outside in the early evening. "If there was a line and you could straddle it like that," Raman uncle continues, "I suppose you'd get shot pretty fast. It's a hostile place, and that would be the price for not knowing to which side you belong."

We all laugh lightly. Besides Raman uncle, the men we are sitting with are all former army officers, and this sort of machismo humor is considered endearing and laughable.

Mitchell and I have spent the day, our last in New Delhi, doing interviews—with assorted strangers on the streets, India's foreign minister at the Capitol Building, some young kids we had found at a popular café/lounge, and finally my great-uncle Prem. After we were done, another uncle of mine and his wife, my mother's sister Meena, had asked us to join them at the "club."

The club is the gymkhana, an old officers compound from the colonial days that I have been visiting ever since I was born. It lies on Race Course Road, India's Pennsylvania Avenue, the same street where much of India's independence movement fifty years ago was mobilized, the same street where India's greatest political freedom fighter, Jawaharlal Nehru, lived and India's greatest spiritual freedom fighter, Mahatma Gandhi, was killed. In fact, from the back lawns of the gymkhana club, you can see the current prime minister's house. In colonial days, the gymkhana club was an elite place, a gathering space for many of the English army officers posted in India. It was the type of place straight out of a Graham Greene novel—an outpost at the edge of the old British empire, fully outfitted with colonial attitude, antiquely furnished ballrooms, finely manicured lawns and tennis courts, libraries full of leather-bound texts from the likes of Chaucer, Oscar Wilde, and Charles Dickens, and well-maintained steamrooms and saunas. In addition, there were cigar bars, where only men were allowed, weekly bridge games arranged exclusively for the wives of officers, and regular formal functions where British officers mixed with guests invited from the outside—Indians.

The strange irony of the place is that fifty years later, not much seems to have changed. Except that the Indian army officers who once served under British superiors now consider the club their own. But they haven't changed the look or the feel of the place. The same lazy green lawns stretch across the grounds, constantly being manicured by young boys. Inside in certain quarters, ties and jackets are required. Brandy and Scotch are still the drinks of choice, and conversations about "parliament's lack of discretion" still linger in the air. Throughout my life, during the long hot summers when we'd visit Delhi, my grandfathers, both Indian military alumni, had brought us to the club. We'd spend all day in the pool or stretched beneath rickety fans, reading comic books. In the evenings we'd run around in the gardens, where dinner was served, and then retreat to dimly lit rooms to play table tennis while the elders sat in the garden and had a drink—or drinks.

And now—at the age of twenty-five—I am sitting for the first time in the garden with the grown-ups. Mitchell and I are about to head off to Kashmir, where we will meet up with the Indian military (Commander Khan and Major Purshottam) in hopes of getting some insight on the war there. I think I am prepared physically and emotionally—not ever having been to a conflict zone—but am curious to know the roots of such wars as the one taking place in Kashmir. Raman uncle—a former Indian military commander who himself has fought in two Indo-Pakistani wars in 1965 and 1971—jokes that besides me, he is the only other family member to go back to Pakistan in fifty-two years—only he went without a visa.

"I wouldn't go at all," my loquacious aunt interrupts. "Those Pakistanis are dogs, killers, with no respect for human life."

In this age of political correctness, such a declaration makes me cringe. I assume it is the product of Indian propaganda and suggest to my aunt that it is likely the Pakistanis feel the same way about Indians.

"Rubbish," she responds. "What do they have to hate? Most of them, I'm sure, secretly still wish they were with India. And the rest—they're the dogs and killers. Trust me, I lived with all of them, among all the Muslims in Kashmir for so many years while your uncle was posted there. I know."

It's tough to argue with such determination. My aunt cannot conceive of any other argument. If another point of view is offered, she purses her lips, shakes her head, and squints her eyes. She's convinced that she is right, no matter how you counterattack. And the more rum she gets in her, the more vociferous she becomes: "How could anyone want to live that way, anyway? The whole place is a wasteland—no culture, color, or God."

In fact, God is the one thing that most Pakistanis claim is the guiding force behind their entire nation. Like many Islamic states, the entire nation is predicated on codified religious law—*sharia*—and is meant to maintain a purity that the rest of the world seems to have lost. To the rest of the world, some of the rituals that go with an Islamic state are odd and unclear. But the nobility of the intention—to maintain a nation that is intrinsically holy—is difficult to question, unless you're an Indian woman with a bit too much rum in you.

"Go ahead, then, see for yourself, they'll make no sense whatever. You'll walk away with more questions than when you entered."

Our first day in Islamabad, Pakistan's capital city, it is 112 degrees Fahrenheit. I feel so lethargic and gross, so overcome by the heat, that I don't want to leave our air-conditioned hotel. I am content to sit in the hotel lobby coffee shop, observe the women who come and go, covered in thick black robes, watch European businessmen dressed in fine suits sit down with Pakistani men dressed in an array of different outfits (traditional robes, Western suits, and collared T-shirts), and make my own judgments. On top of it, though, I may not be willing to voice this emotion, I am afraid. Prior to our departure, we saw and heard the warnings from the U.S. State Department—Pakistan is listed as hostile territory for all American travelers. Practically speaking, an official from the State Department told us that it was okay to go but that we should consider ourselves, in his words "targets," and we should always be aware of our surroundings. Mitch, who has visited Pakistan as well as Afghanistan several times in the last few years, backs this up, instructing me that we should always be conscious of crowds gathering around us, always be alert and aware of an escape route in a crowded place, and never argue with any interview subject—especially a young man.

I seldom go places to do stories without some element of fear inside me. I consider it a healthy way of keeping myself alert to where I am, and whom I'm with, and an insurance mechanism to keep me from doing something wholly stupid. But the fear I am facing in Pakistan is different. It stems from confusion, not only about whom I'm going out to talk to, but who it is that I am myself. I feel I am wearing two badges in particular—I am American, I am Indian—and neither is welcome in this strange place. I recall Commander Khan's words back in Kashmir.

"They're just like us," he had said, waving his gun at the border somewhere off in the distance. "They point. They shoot. They kill. For every Indian they kill, there's one less enemy to deal with. There's one less boy out there shooting for them—whether or not they're holding a gun. Be careful."

If that isn't enough to be apprehensive about, the all too familiar image of rowdy crowds of young boys burning American flags is stamped in my head. Who should I be today? I wonder. The American or the Indian? Who is more likely to be the object of fury?

Beyond these fears, I can also feel something else pulling at me—a responsibility, an obligation, to go out and find these villains. Unlike some of our other trips where a general vendetta is in play, this one feels different, more personal somehow. This time I am told I am the target, and I want to see for myself who is targeting me. . . . But maybe it's all bullshit, the product of American and anti-Islamic propaganda. Maybe I'll discover that there is nothing to be afraid of out there in the stifling heat. So off we go.

We spend the afternoon out and about, first interviewing a retired army general in his office—his medals and ribbons regally adorning the walls behind him. He seems alarmed when we tell him we have no need to film them. How can we do a story on war if we aren't interested in the badges and outfits that go along with it?

In response, I tell him that something is bothering me. Earlier in our conversation he had told me stories of his involvement in the Indo-Pakistani wars of 1965 and 1971. Just a few days earlier, I had listened to stories from Raman uncle about the same wars—but from the other side. I have realized it is possible that these two gentlemen at one time in those two wars may have faced off against each other, each poised to pull the trigger and kill the other. It seems odd that in the course of a few days I have been chatting with both, sharing drinks and tea and talking about the same wars. I inform him of this.

"Don't be alarmed, young man," the general says to me in an avuncular tone. "War does funny things. I'm quite sure if the circumstances were different I would share a cup of tea or a meal with your uncle. We might chat about our similar backgrounds—not understand how we're supposed to be enemies. Our fathers [both of whom were in the Indian military] may have done so at the club fifty years ago. One moment friends, the next foes. You learn to live with it."

And so the afternoon passes. At one point in the early evening Mitch and I make our way to a small town that I have been told is the site of my grandfather's medical school. We search the streets for almost an hour but can't find it. Instead, we find ourselves wandering up a busy road in the town of Rawalpindi. We do indeed draw crowds of people around us, young men in droves peering in at the camera and at us. When they ask me where I am from, I resolve a new answer that carefully avoids admitting being Indian or American.

"My grandparents are from Pakistan," I mutter with an awkward smile.

And the men around us nod, seemingly indifferent to my carefully crafted response. They are more curious about the camera—as if America somehow resides inside the lens. For myself, I keep looking for familiar landmarks wherever we go. Though I have never been to Pakistan, I am convinced that something I'll see will bring out some sort of genetic memory in me handed down from my ancestors.

We have spent close to ten days amid the war, stalking the hills of Kashmir, prowling streets and offices in Delhi, and so far a day wandering in Pakistan. For the purposes of our story, most of the players have revealed themselves. We have interviewed politicians and civilians on both sides, as well as officers in the military, and even had a chance to speak with some young soldiers on the Indian side. One set of characters, however, remains elusive. For close to two decades, Indians have complained loudly that the violence up and around Kashmir is the result of militancy launched by Islamic terrorists trained, sponsored, and sent over from Pakistan. Pakistan has vehemently denied these charges and states that though it does "diplomatically, politically, and spiritually" support the independence movement in Kashmir, it does not actively or militarily support it. In this way, a high-stakes "yes, you are—no, we're not" squabble has endured for almost twenty years. The acrimony is sharp and constant, and in its midst, thousands are dying.

In my few days covering this story, I have become convinced that the boys fighting for freedom in Kashmir are lurking in Pakistan. We have been told about training camps—some of them housed in *madrasas,* or religious schools, in both Pakistan and Afghanistan, where young Islamic boys are taught how to use weapons like grenades, handguns, antiaircraft guns, and other heavy artillery. Our primary goal in Pakistan is to find one of these places and one of the "students" who attend it. How we were going to do that, we aren't entirely sure.

I imagine that the best way to find out which young boys may be fighting in the war is simply to locate some and ask. So we head for a little strip mall we find on the side of the road and wander through the interior. Outside a small Internet café, we find a group of young men—four boys all in their twenties, hanging out, sharing some cigarettes, trading some stories, and laughing heartily. They nod and smile at us as we walk toward them and invite us for a smoke.

We chat briefly. Two of them are students, and the others work in a neighboring shop as software designers. I tell them who we are, where we have been, and what we are doing.

"You've been to Kashmir?" one of them remarks, raising his eyebrows.

Yes.

"They're murdering our boys there." He shakes his head and takes a deep drag on his cigarette.

So they're coming from here?

"Of course," says another one, laughing, "the politicians you've spoken to deny it, yeah?"

And of course, earlier in the day a Pakistani official we spoke to did just that.

"But we see them going one after another, one after another, our friends."

Mitch asks about the infamous *madrasas,* if there are any around where we can go to find the young men who someday will leave for Kashmir.

One of the boys toward the back, who is eyeing us studiously and silently, murmurs something. I look at him.

"Why go there?" he repeats himself. "You've found one here."

His friends drop their smiles and nod. Now that he has broken confidentiality, they are free to acknowledge his admission.

His name is Amir, and he reveals that he has spent close to three months at a *madrasa* in Afghanistan—rumored by the U.S. State Department to be the place where Osama bin Laden has been for years holed up training legions of young men in combat. Then he lists the various weapons he was trained to handle—assorted guns, grenades, poisonous gases, antiaircraft artillery, knives.

"Full-on training hand-to-hand combat also," he notes. "You know, in case you end up face-to-face with your enemy, you'll know how to handle him."

Just as we are intrigued by his stories, they are fascinated by the fact that Mitchell and I have just been in Kashmir days before. "What does it look like?" they want to know. "Is it really as beautiful as everyone describes it?"

They are completely unfamiliar with the place they are willing to die for. It is a unique sort of commitment, both noble and stupid at the same time.

"How about India?" Amir inquires. "What are the young people like there? Are they like us, willing to die?"

It is a tough question to answer. When I think of the young people I know in India—my own cousins—I think of a fairly decadent and materialistic lot who would rather spend an evening at a disco than talk about political and military affairs in some remote part of their country. In that way, they are profoundly similar to young people all over the world, including Pakistan, where these guys too would rather talk about girls and movies. The difference, however, is that they manage simultaneously to have a unique determination hidden inside them, the wherewithal to keep fighting even if they aren't exactly sure of their enemy. Not one of the four of them has ever been to India. And they have no desire to go.

"Not until it is broken into pieces. Shattered by us . . . *Inshalla*." One of Amir's friends smiles as he invokes the Islamic expression translated as "God willing."

How about me? My parents are Indian and I am American. I'm of Hindu background. You are obviously Islamic. Should we not be enemies?

"Oh, but we are." Amir smiles back at me, unfazed by my question. "Enemies and friends at the same time. Friends here"—he signals to the ground beneath us with his fist and then raises it, waving—"and enemies there."

Amir takes a deep hit of his cigarette and offers it to me— I shake my head. "Share a smoke here on this side of the line and be friends. Cross over . . . enemies."

He nods at me. "I have been trained to kill. And were I to go to Kashmir . . . and I will, *Inshalla* . . . you will be my enemy. And my commander will tell me to kill you, and I will. Slit your throat—I've been trained to—without hesitation. Kill a friend because he is my enemy."

I would have expected steely eyes to enhance the drama of his words, but he just keeps nodding with hardly the intimidation of a fifteen-year-old basketball player on the playgrounds of New York. There is no complication as far as he is concerned—friends and foes at the same time.

Soon after, Mitch and I climb back into our car and head for the hotel. We have achieved what we set out to do—we have found one of the terrorists and interviewed him. But I don't feel good—I feel sick.

I want to go. I want to leave this place. I want to leave Pakistan.

Mitch agrees. We have done what we set out to do. We make one more stop on the way back to the hotel so our driver can fill up the car with gas. While we wait, I climb a small hill overlooking the city and admire the beautiful Islamic architecture along the flat land just in front of a ridge of mountains that form the range that leads to Kashmir. The hot zone is literally some anti-Shangri-la hidden in their midst. I have come to Pakistan hoping on behalf of my family to rediscover some familiarity from the place that we have come from. But it isn't there.

When I had asked Prem uncle if he had ever returned to Lahore since that day he had evacuated, he said no. I had asked him if he envisioned a trip soon, dreamed of going back—for in relatively peaceful times, it is quite possible nowadays. "I dream of it every day," he had said. It was the closest in our conversation he had come to tears.

And for that reason, I hadn't pushed it. I hadn't asked why in fifty-two years he had not gone back, taken a week or two to make the trip from Delhi to Lahore, once sister-cities that are about the distance between New York City and Boston.

But standing up on the hill, I feel I have my answer. There is no home left. There is nothing to come back to. Whatever it is that was once home no longer exists in this place. Prem uncle knows it without seeing it for himself. Too many horrifying images are linked with his last hours there. Friends transformed to enemies—neighbors to killers. Or maybe, as Amir has said, they had always been playing both roles at the same time. The world, their world just exposed them—their darker faces seen for a few moments, the startling images of which will now last an eternity.

It isn't until almost twelve hours later, sitting on the airplane headed home to the United States, that something Amir said comes to the forefront of my consciousness about his training and the hand-to-hand combat skills he had learned: "You know, in case you end up face-to-face with your enemy, you'll know how to handle him." In a quite literal way, these were surely skills that may have enabled him in battle. But, I wonder, what if you aren't sure who your enemy is? What if your enemy today is your friend yesterday or tomorrow? Will you be able to recognize him then, even face-to-face?

When India and Pakistan divorced years ago, they left in their wake millions of jilted lovers—lovers whose romance was no longer possible. And as happens with any relationship that turns sour, the two parties—in this case Indians and Pakistanis—retreated, angry and bitter, and with soft, hidden hints of sadness. I have left Pakistan only once in my life, and initially when I looked back at it, I felt deep conflict in my heart. Time has brought some clarity, however. I now realize that it was never Pakistan that disappointed me or fell below expectations, but rather my own refusal and inability to come to grips with what the reality of the place is. I had hoped to carry Prem uncle's eyes with me and perhaps to reclaim some part of his home, my own heritage. But that wasn't possible, and that made me angry. Pakistan has been rebuilt without Prem uncle's permission, without my permission. Now there are boys like Amir walking around readjusting the entire meaning of existence.

And now when I think about it, I find a unique message delivered by the most unlikely messenger.

Amir, in his own way, had discovered the same essential truth that Siddhartha Buddha did traveling the holy cities of ancient India. He had discovered, perhaps without realizing it, that all things are impermanent—even the roles that we play— the same truth that Prem uncle continues to live through to this day. Yesterday a friend, tomorrow a foe, and today—the gray zone, the no-man's-land where all of us perilously wait for our newest role to be revealed. It's a tough way to live, especially when one does it with such intense intimacy, with such painful scars, the way Prem uncle does.

A sharp-witted and intellectual man, Prem uncle wasted little time establishing a new life in Delhi. He didn't marry until the age of fifty, when he finally wed a woman twenty-five years younger than he was. They never had children. Instead they looked after the rest of the family—especially his sister Bimla, widowed at the age of twenty-five with two young boys.

My grandmother tells me that Bimla auntie never fully healed from losing her husband. I never met her because she died at the age of sixty-eight from a rare form of Lou Gehrig's disease. As she lay in her hospital bed for close to a year, her young niece sat by her bedside religiously. A young doctor— still in his final year of medical school—was assigned as the attending physician, and when he was done with his rounds, he'd stop by one last time in Bimla auntie's room. Even in her dying days, Bimla auntie knew why.

My mother says my father would look over the charts mechanically—for he had seen them just hours before—and then loiter around, chatting away with her about silly things like the Beatles and that thing sweeping across America and the world—rock & roll. And Bimla auntie, on a respirator (imported especially from London by Prem uncle) and too weak near the end to say much, would squeeze her hand happily as the clock ticked and the young doctor continued to stay.

My parents got married in the spring of 1971—two weeks after Bimla auntie passed. Unlike most Indian weddings, which are loud, drunken, celebratory affairs, Mom and Papa's was in the morning, small and soft—the way Bimla auntie was.

In my own way, out of all of this, I suppose I've created some sort of fantasy to qualify myself as one of Salman Rushdie's "midnight's children." If Prem uncle had not endured his fate, perhaps I would have never seen mine. If India and Pakistan had not split, Indir uncle (Prem uncle's brother-in-law) might not have been killed. Bimla auntie might not have moved to Delhi. She would not have died in a New Delhi hospital wing assigned to a young physician, and the fateful encounter between my parents would never have come to pass. Life itself is built on a mountain of ifs. One man's scar can be another's womb.

Hung Over

I am sitting outside on the corner of 55th Street and Sixth Avenue. It's about three A.M. I come here often late after a night spent downtown in the trendy bars of Manhattan's elite or the dank interiors of taverns and cafés that all New Yorkers consider their own. Sometimes I bring my little dog, since she likes the smell of the pushcarts that cook *halal* meat sandwiches as much as I do. We sit on the stone surface of the fountain outside the huge Price Waterhouse skyscraper, buy a three-dollar sandwich, and enjoy one last taste of today before it fades into tomorrow.

It's mostly men who gather on this corner. They're not locals—usually young taxi drivers from Brooklyn and Queens, an assortment of dark guys who speak fast in Farsi or Urdu and enjoy the skittering music that rattles out of a busted transistor on the top of the food stand. They come from various places—Egypt, Iran, Syria, Pakistan, and Afghanistan—and though their respective cultures are distinct, they've formed a remarkable fraternity that is unique in a city of twelve million strangers.

I am often mistaken as one of them. They salute me as one of their own, *salaam alekham.* And sometimes I fake a familiar response.

Asalaam alekham.

But if the conversation goes any further, I am revealed and their expressions turn from confused to humorous. They are friendly just the same. It is I who feel left out, because I'm not in on their jokes, barbs, and expressions.

Reza is one of the guys who run the stalls. On most nights he's a nonstop machine, chopping up chicken and mixing it with sliced aromatic peppers, onions, and chilies; slicing off thin sheets of lamb for gyro sandwiches or platters. This man knows his trade and crafts a meal with an alarming alacrity, yet with the diligence of an engineer building a complex model by hand.

But tonight is a slow night, and a line of four or five men barely keeps Reza at his usual post. He retreats back to the fountain where I am sitting and takes a seat beside me.

We start chatting—Reza is from Pakistan.

"Really?" I tell him that I have just returned from there.

He's thrilled and asks me if I am from there as well.

"No." But am quick to add out of habit that my grandparents were. I note this internally as a curious fear-filled habit that is okay to break now.

"India?" Reza asks, still with the same excited smile on his face.

"Yes."

"Same thing."

Ironic, judging by the past few days spent half a world away.

Reza's twenty-six. He's been in this country seven years. Business is good, but he thinks he needs a change. He's like any twentysomething picking and choosing professions as though they're different fruits dangling from one tree.

"Everyone likes to do different things," he says. "Why wear one face when it's only natural to wear many?"

It's a funny expression, I think. But Pakistanis, who often speak a variety of lyrical and poetic languages like Urdu, Pashto, Punjabi, and others, use expressions translated from their great ancient musical and poetic traditions.

I give him a quizzical look, and he resorts to more familiar and mundane analogies. "Americans"—his mouth spreads into a wide, toothy grin—"*we* like to say there is black and there is white and there are many shades of gray. All of us wander in and out of all the different shades."

Somehow what he is saying works, and it makes me think of my time in India, in Kashmir, in Pakistan, among brothers born of the same womb, now sworn enemies seeking each other's blood. I think of Amir, somewhere on the other side of the world—if even he is still alive—hunting and being hunted by enemies and friends.

If he saw me now, this moment, sitting beside one of his countrymen, casually talking in riddles, metaphors, and esoteric terms because we are not faced with the immediate horrors of his world, what might he think?

We talk briefly about the war in Kashmir, Reza and I. He's familiar with it, as he lived close to Islamabad, and claims to know boys who trained in the *madrasas*. He might have been one of them, if things had worked out differently, he notes with no trace of irony. He says he's angry about the war and probably won't go back until it's resolved.

My sandwich is done, and some of the others have wandered to their own spaces, engaged in conversation. The two of us sit, inheritors of a strange and silent moment—both of us contemplating the same war from different, yet similar, perspectives.

"War," he says, and frowns. "Why? Indians and Pakistanis—brothers, neighbors." He pats me on the back. "One day, maybe I will go home, when there is peace. Maybe then," he says almost longingly as he gets back up to tend to a new customer, *"Inshalla."*

Las Terroristas and HBO

Free of the constraints of mind and body, Buddha found that he had not reached an ending but had instead arrived at a beginning. Enlightenment and freedom were not about personal deliverance. He felt a sudden vocation to take his knowledge and teach it to others. True enlightenment was not in personal elevation, but in the ability to reach out, to offer compassion to a world desperate for it, and raise others' awareness.

Compassion

Several months ago, while visiting my parents in California, I found myself aimlessly going through the bookshelves in their bedroom. Wedged in among hundreds of other books, I found an intriguing old text. The binding was scratched and a few of the pages torn. It was a science book circa 1970 that surely must have been uncovered at a local used-book store. I took it down, sat on the couch, and began to flip through it.

Inside there were a few remedial sketches of simple experiments conducted years ago. One in particular caught my attention. Three boxed sketches were lined up, one on top of the next. In the first, a small mouse has been placed in an empty, sealed, transparent container. From the text the reader learns that within a few days, the mouse, having used all the available oxygen, suffocates and dies. In sketch number two, a plant is placed in the same sealed container and within days the same fate ensues. In box number three, both the mouse and the plant are placed in the sealed container. But now the two of them survive and, judging by the sketch, seem to live happily ever after.

It's not an entirely mind-blowing experiment—the science is fairly easy to explain. Alone, both the mouse and the plant use up all the available air and die when it runs out. Together, they exchange the required oxygen and carbon dioxide and survive off of each other. It's simple and rather cool—their only chance at survival is in their relationship with one another. Simply put, *life is a relationship.*

Day One

I write to you from Continental Airlines flight 1006, or from Houston to Bogotá. We're presently about 2½ hours away from touching down in Colombia's capital city. Our plan is to be there for about two weeks—*two weeks*—covering a story on the United States's involvement in the training of Colombian "counternarcotics brigades," which combat the production and trafficking of drugs to the United States. I've been trying to soften the idea of spending two weeks in one of the most dangerous places in the world by telling myself it's really only twelve days. I concluded this just moments ago, since we arrive there rather late tonight and leave early in the morning thirteen nights from now. You see what I mean?

I only received this assignment several days ago. I was in Cleveland, sitting in a bar and talking to a bartender named Choker, readying myself to be trained by a fifteen-year-old girl at an NRA gun camp the following day, when my pager started to vibrate. When I called the office, they told me.

"Get ready to go to Colombia."

Ever since then I've had a strange feeling and I haven't entirely figured out what it is. I have, however, started to suspect. . . . Two nights ago, I woke up in a cold sweat. I could not recall any of my dreams, but my sheets were soaked. I got up and started watching television—a replay of Mötley Crüe in *Behind the Music* on VH1.

Last night I awoke at four in the morning, just like that, and never managed to get back to sleep. I spent the remainder of the night counting how many more starts Pedro Martinez would make this season for my beloved Red Sox. How many more games, assuming he won all of his, would we have to win to clinch the wild-card spot in the playoffs?

And then there was the airport in Houston. I felt a tugging urgency to call my mother even when they were making the final boarding call for my flight. Even though I knew I could call her from Colombia in a few hours, I still wanted to call from the safe harbor of the United States. And my girlfriend in New York: I knew she was at work and I couldn't reach her, so instead I had some flowers sent to her. I can't explain why—I don't think I really want to.

The ubiquitous threat in Colombia seems to be kidnapping. The Marxist guerrillas and the leftist paramilitary forces both, in part, finance their existence by kidnapping and extorting huge sums of money. I've been advised not to use my surname, as dad's books have been best-sellers in Colombia and he has achieved a certain notoriety. In general, however, Americans are regarded as hot property. The jury is still out as to whether journalists have any immunity from these kidnappings.

Two young Americans are sitting beside me: Amanda and Bill. Ever since they sat down I've been wondering what in God's name would pull them down to this treacherous part of the world. I asked them politely over dinner. Of course, it turns out, it is ironically enough, indeed, God's name that draws them south.

"We're missionaries." Amanda smiles. Both of them are twenty-two.

"Surely you're aware of the danger," I say.

"Of course, *las terroristas*," Amanda says. She pauses, but her thin face doesn't show a hint of fear. "Just over a year ago, three Americans like us—volunteers in one of the villages—there to help the village people, were abducted, charged with being sympathizers, and executed."

Bill is silent. His face is pale and placid—I think, like me, he is scared by not knowing what this place looks like.

"But," Amanda picks up, "we come from a place of compassion, from a place of sharing. Not that they didn't," she quickly adds. "They paid the ultimate price for their compassion, their desire to save the innocents. I hope that provides some measure of insurance, either in this life or the next."

She smiles. To me, Bill looks as if he wants to vomit.

Frankly, I don't care much for Amanda's spiritual allegiance or intentions, but I applaud her courage. I wish them well, and they do the same.

Erin Brockovich with Julia Roberts is playing in the main

cabin. Strange, I think, how this movie has preceded me the past few weeks into uncertain places, Iran and now Colombia. I think I'll watch the ending—the happy ending.

Ninety minutes until arrival. . . .

Day Two—Bogotá

Although Colombia has been called the most dangerous place in the Western Hemisphere, you wouldn't get that impression from walking around the square just outside my hotel window. The streets are lined with upscale bars. After office hours these are packed with young, attractive men and women pouring down drink after drink. All three nights we've been here, we've managed to go out and try a different café—I've rediscovered my taste for Cuba libres.

If I could simplify the story down here in Colombia, it would be reduced to this—in the United States, we have over the past few years reached ever higher levels of drug consumption. Eighty percent of the drugs consumed in the United States come from Colombia. So this year the U.S. government decided to tackle the problem at the source: They pledged $1.6 billion specifically for the training of antinarco brigades, who venture off into the jungle to eradicate the poppy and coca fields that happen to be protected by a heavily armed guerrilla group known as the FARC (Revolutionary Armed Forces of Colombia).

Today we met a young journalist named Alejandro. I hoped that he could simplify the story for us so that we could figure out a way to tell it to our audience.

"Gotham," he addressed me when I told him our goal, "it is anything but simple here in Colombia. The one thing I can tell you is that the problem exists only because it is a shared one. The lifeblood for this war comes from the United States. Everything is interrelated. It's the only way for the war to survive."

I mentioned my journey to Sri Lanka, where the war endures simply because of an indifference that seems to pervade the general consciousness.

"Yes, the war is like that here as well, I suppose." Alejandro nodded. "But here, it's not about religion or ethnicity or such things, it's about money—pure and simple. People here share one desire—to have wealth and therefore have power."

Though the strength of the drug cartels has dropped during the last decade, the flood of money from the drug trade has not waned. The cocaine and heroin grown all over Colombia are more in demand today than ever before. The rebel guerrilla group known as the FARC has for years levied a tax on the narco-traffickers who subsidize farmers growing the poppy seeds and coca plants that serve as the raw ingredients of the drugs cocaine and heroin. Though they insist they are not involved directly in the production or trafficking of drugs, the FARC is hugely dependent on the drug trade as the money they collect from the actual traffickers generates millions of dollars per month. When this source of income is threatened, the FARC is known for their very violent ways—the frequent obliteration of villages and slaughtering of village people who do not pledge their allegiance to them. Their second major source of revenue is kidnapping, nabbing Colombians and foreigners alike and then charging no less than $1 million apiece in ransom.

The Colombian government is now in its fourth decade of fighting the FARC. And to complicate matters even more, an extremist group known as the paramilitary, or the "death squads," which lurk all over the country, participating in massacres or the kidnapping of those they consider sympathetic to the rebel FARC.

The result is a messy three-way civil war and a nation ripped apart by violence, murder, and fear.

Day Three

Today's been pretty easy, with not much to do besides plan for leaving Bogotá tomorrow. I went for a walk through the square earlier in the day and enjoyed the sun. Despite the danger, people here have managed to carry on with their lives. In a way this is a shame, because it normalizes the horror and perpetuates it. But I realize this is an idealistic way to look at things. In reality, people here have no choice but to carry on. From that vantage point, the older gentlemen sitting at the corners, reading the papers and talking with one another about the state of politics in the Balkans, are supremely admirable. Their fearlessness is defiance. They thumb their noses at any who try to intimidate them.

I take a seat beside them, order a fruit drink, and determine to just sit there for a while and watch the moderate traffic on the road in front of the café. City buses roll by intermittently, packed to capacity with passengers—mostly young men. Staring at these buses as they pass, I realize that they are very much like the jammed city buses I've seen in other parts of the world—India, Pakistan, and Iran, to name a few.

They move through the cities like bloated dragons—commuter buses jammed to capacity, with still more people pouring out of the doorways, hanging on to poles, windows, whatever seems sturdy. In India, these buses roll down the city streets spewing thick black clouds of exhaust that refuse to rise up into the sky but instead sink in the intolerable heat.

When I was young, my grandparents forbade us from riding the city buses because of the danger. Though cumulatively I had spent years in India, until I was twenty-five years old I had still never ridden on one of the buses, remaining bound by my grandparents' orders.

So several months ago, when my producer, Mitch, and I were in Pakistan and he recommended we grab on to a bus and ride it for a few blocks, I felt a surge of energy. The buses in Pakistan are as torturous as any in India or the ones passing me here in Bogotá—packed to at least three times capacity and filled almost entirely with men. Though I had never tried it, I had watched many men try—and some fail—to board the buses. It seemed to me that the most successful technique was to run alongside the bus just as it started to roll from its last stop. That way a passenger could grab on to whatever space was available and let the momentum of the vehicle pull him in. It was risky—failure meant that a prospective passenger could spill out from the moving vehicle into the crowded street. Though I had never seen it happen, my cousins and I had heard stories from our grandparents about young boys who had been killed when they fell from the buses and were struck by the rushing traffic.

But that day in Pakistan it seemed to me it would be a cultural experience, like running with the bulls in Pamplona, Spain. I felt I was ready to take my shot.

We spotted a bus lumbering down the center of the street. As I've said, the rules do not say that you can board only at a bus stop. In fact, it is when the bus halts in the middle of traffic, at a light, or for whatever other reason that the activity begins. The bus starts to look like a gently moving anthill—men pouring in and out of the narrow doorways and aisles and then hanging on for dear life as it pulls away.

Mitch had done this twenty-five years ago or so, in the

midst of a post-hippie transcontinental journey that included stopovers in Iran, Turkey, Pakistan, and other such locales. It seemed nostalgic to him somehow, the way he rushed from the street corner without looking back, his camera held tightly in his hand. I myself was hesitant, drumming up the courage to first dance through the traffic in order to even get to the bus.

But Mitch was already running alongside the bus, scanning for an opening along the doorway, then leaping up agilely, catching hold of the smallest, most microscopic sliver of rusted metal railing, and wedging himself between the malleable bodies.

By that time, I was running along the side of the bus itself. The traffic light ahead had turned green and the cacophony of horns was deafening. As the bus lurched into second gear, I was still unable to see any opening where I might fit.

But the side of the road was now an impossibility, as traffic had picked up. I was like a castaway lost at sea, within view of a coastline that would never again be reached.

Now the bus was ready to hit third gear. Mitch was looking around anxiously, trying to push back and create an opening for me. At this stage, my only option was to go for it.

I couldn't believe it, it flashed in my head, here in Pakistan amid the Mujahadeen, a Hindu among Muslims, an American amid antagonists, and my downfall would come like this— falling from a bus like an amateur rodeo rider. So on faith alone I leapt, jutting my arm into a mash of bodies, searching for something, anything, inside to grab and hang on to.

And there was nothing—nothing but ragged shirts and tattered pants unable to sustain the weight of my pull. I felt myself falling back, falling out onto the road. Frantically I wiggled my hand in a last effort to find anything that might save me.

But it was not happening. . . .

Then, suddenly, I felt a hand lock on to my forearm. There

was no way to see inside where this salvation was coming from, but there I was aboard the bus, fixed into place because of an anonymous gift of security, a hand reaching out, reeling me in, and hauling me safely inside.

Day Four

You cannot drive through the Colombian countryside, so although the place we are headed is less than a hundred miles south of Bogotá, we board a rickety twin-prop plane and climb into the air. I have heard that in Colombia, domestic planes are on occasion hijacked and all the passengers taken captive and held for ransom. Trying not to think of this, I dive into the *Batman* comic book I picked up at the airport.

The first stop we make is in a small airfield in the village of Neive. I recall the name of the town from one of the young college students I spoke to in Bogotá—"We feel relatively safe in Bogotá compared with a place like Neive, where people are murdered every day."

I stare at my watch, counting the seconds until the plane lifts off once more.

When we touch down in San Vicente, we have arrived in rebel territory. As opposed to a place like Neive, which is technically government-controlled territory and therefore shared and conflicted territory, San Vicente is part of the 40 percent of Colombia that has been ceded by the Colombian government to various rebel groups—most of it going to the FARC.

And it's noticeable. The airport is far more rudimentary. The flags flying over the main building and the little ones blowing atop the taxicabs are not Colombian, they are FARC. Whether or not they truly believe in the FARC—and that is in question—the local people pledge at least a superficial allegiance to the rebels. Not to do so is a pledge with death.

Our "fixer" directs us to a taxi driver he knows. This is important because getting into a taxi with someone you don't know can lead to a ride directly to a safe house, where you end up spending the remainder of your fear-filled life. But it's hard to imagine Lalo, our driver, as such an insidious person. He smiles jovially and keeps nodding his head, repeating the word *welcome*. He also decides to call me Gato, or "cat," because he can't pronounce my name.

We head directly for the main town square and the central FARC office, where we start lobbying for a chance to head into the jungle and meet with one of the various FARC commanders. Inside the barren concrete office we wait . . . and wait . . . and wait, until finally a young woman dressed in fatigues with an AK hanging over her shoulder brings us some bottled water, smiles, and asks us to . . . wait.

And we do wait for a few more hours. After a while, I stop looking at my watch, remembering that in Bogotá Alejandro had told us that the FARC simply have a completely different standard of time. This is why thirty-five years of war is like nothing to them. This is why holding a hostage for a year or two before even making a ransom demand is routine. They are patient beyond definition.

Finally, sometime in the evening hours, the same woman sporting the same gun but with an additional American-made army vest strapped with grenades pokes her head through the doorway and says that the radio is not working. They're having no luck contacting the base camp outside of the town.

She says that we should head to our hotel for the night. She recommends that early in the morning we head directly to the camp and promises that she'll try again to let them know we are coming. There seems to be no reasonable alternative, so we comply and head for the Hotel Marina, where we have deluxe rooms reserved.

My *deluxe* room at the Hotel Marina is a seven-foot-by-seven-foot plain walled box with a bed and bath. The bathroom is not even separated by a door to the main room. In other words, the can has a beautiful and direct view of the bed.

My room, however, is truly plush compared with that of my producer, Chris's, who is situated at the end of the complex. He has only a six-inch wall separating him from the street, where a minimum of six different cafés are blaring jarring local music. It's so loud that you can't have a normal conversation in his room. He shouts at me to be ready by five-thirty A.M. so we can leave. I nod my head and retreat.

Day Five

Driving through the countryside within San Vicente, you cannot help but notice the beauty. We're not that far from the Amazon jungle, so the land is lush, thick, and green. The rugged road that cuts through the jungles winds around small hills. In the valleys sit static pillows of clouds. There are animals—cows, donkeys, horses, and ponies—wandering the roads and the valleys, and all are marked with a brand that identifies them as belonging to the FARC. There are also small signs nailed on trees that request us in Spanish not to pollute the water, cut the trees, or throw out garbage. They're all sponsored by the FARC. It's interesting that they seem to be environmentally conscious.

After driving about half an hour, we come to the first FARC

roadblock. Lalo turns and smiles, *no worry, no worry,* but my nerves kick in nevertheless. It's been rumored that FARC rebels at the roadblocks will often pull out an attractive kidnapping candidate. If the passenger is Colombian, the FARC have been known to pull out a computer gadget in which they can scan the name and see how much money the prospective kidnappee has in his or her bank account. And foreigners, although they make for potentially messy political situations, are also potentially lucrative.

We sit as Lalo explains something to the AK-wielding rebel peering into the car. I'm not listening closely but hear a few words—"Christian," "Brian," my crewmates' names, and also "Gato."

The rebel bends and taps on the window with the barrel of the gun. I roll it down and stare out at him. He looks in at us, packed in the backseat with our camera equipment. His eyes seem suspicious to me. I drop my eyes. After a few minutes he lets us pass.

I exhale, relieved. But was he really looking at us suspiciously? I can't help but wonder. Or was it that I was suspicious of him? Or was it both of us, projecting some divisive line, sharing some anxiety about the foreign flavor of the other unsure how to communicate?

Any time you cross over to the other side and meet with rebel forces, the day is logged into your personal diary as a historic moment. Here you are, willingly walking into hostile territory—which is like willingly walking down the end of the pirate's plank, hoping that the imminent plunge will be a pretty swan dive rather than an execution.

Our timing, of course, is rather provocative, and we know it. Two nights prior, a young Scottish traveler who had been kidnapped months earlier had reportedly been executed by the FARC. And just the day before, twenty-nine university students, including an American professor, had been kidnapped in one of the northern cities. As it turns out, these kidnappers are not FARC, but another rebel group. But any time kidnappings and, of course, executions occur, all of the militant groups come under increased scrutiny. Under any circumstances, and especially these, there is no certainty that we will have any luck in obtaining an interview.

Lalo has brought us as far as he can, up a dirt road to a barbed-wired fence and an opening beside which a dilapidated wooden guard post hangs together. Inside, two young soldiers sit, their faces blank. One of them is shirtless, a thin scar cutting across his upper torso. Lalo approaches them and rattles off something in Spanish. The bare-chested rebel mutters something back, and Lalo turns to us, nods, and then steps through the gate and disappears down another gravelly road. Within moments he returns with a burly, fatigue-covered fellow who introduces himself as Jim. He smiles, turns and waves the back of his hand at us, and begins to walk.

Camps like this one are literally the last Marxist outposts in the world, and they seem to exist in some sort of time warp. Walking in from the outside is jarring. Jim, like the young rebels in the guard post, is difficult to read. His gaze is sterile. Physically his face is bushy-browed and his expression placid. Like everyone around us, he has some sort of automatic weapon hanging from his shoulder. We are introduced to a phalanx of similarly outfitted guerrillas, each of whom shakes hands, mumbles a few things in Spanish, and moves on.

Finally we're shown a small area covered with a banana-leafed, thatched roof. "Wait, *aquí*," Jim orders us politely. "*Voy a regresar* soon."

An hour passes. Two hours pass. I finish the copy of *High Fidelity* I had stuffed into one of my pockets.

Three hours pass. A young female militant brings us frigid bottles of mineral water, smiles, and leaves.

Could this be the definition of waiting for death? I wonder. We resort to office gossip.

She slept with who?

That's why he had an affair.

I knew he was gay.

Four hours pass. I admit to stopping occasionally on the radio dial when I hear a Backstreet Boys or Britney Spears song.

Brian, our cameraman, admits a liking for Christina Aguilera.

Enrique Iglesias earned respect from Chris after an appearance on Howard Stern.

Our fixer has a thing for Ricky Martin.

Closing in on the fifth hour, Jim returns. He nods and says, "Come."

There reportedly are rebel camps scattered all over Colombia. Rendezvous with FARC commanders are always last minute. They notoriously wander between the jungles and the hills, rarely sleeping in the same camp on consecutive nights. Internally there are factions in the FARC, and even the most veteran journalists in Colombia have trouble breaking down and explaining the hierarchies, tensions, and conflicts among the different commanders.

"Be careful whom you mention in conversation. One commander may not like another one. It can get messy."

I have had my fill of my own office gossip and have no need to get involved in theirs.

We make our way down some dirt trails, pushing brush from in front of our faces. We emerge in a clearing, plunge through it, and wade through the thick jungle once more.

Finally we arrive.

Another cluster of young FARC rebels is there to greet us. More guns—Russian-made AKs, American M16s and strapped Colt 45s, Israeli-made Galils.

There's no hint of the nature of what we'll see or with whom we might be talking. I am fed more names, and more greeting hands are outstretched. I shake them amicably, as if I am at a state dinner in the White House.

"Okay, come," Jim intones.

We move through a moderate-size jungle camp—green tents tied between trees, pails, more guns, and fatigues, all hanging loosely here and there. I am reminded of *M*A*S*H.*

Then Jim pulls back the opening to another tent, and standing there is a small man dressed in green fatigues.

"Commander Rios," Jim announces.

It comes with such subtle drama that I feel as if I should be in front of Fidel Castro. Ivan Rios is one of the FARC commanders. He's known as an articulate man, unlike some of the other extremists and hardened militant commanders. In addition, Rios's eyes are soft, and for an organization with such a violent reputation, there is something truly uncanny about this. There's strength in his gaze—a look of sincerity. *He's pleased to meet me,* and I believe him.

I ask him if we might sit and talk for a while so he can explain some things about the FARC.

"Sit." He nods.

Maybe outside, I refer to the camera. Light.

He looks at the camera suspiciously, as if it is some sort of intruder.

Porqué?

I explain once again who we are, what our gig is, and so on. He relents. We make our way outside.

He notices that I am limping and asks with concern if I have hurt myself in Colombia.

No, I explain that I hurt myself a few weeks ago playing basketball at home in New York.

"Good," he says, and then stutters as he tries to backtrack and explain that he is happy only that I have not sustained the injury in Colombia.

I nod and smile back.

We make our way to a clearing beside some tents. Some of the young guerrillas look at us passing but don't come too close. I notice beneath one large tent a group of young rebels watching a TV connected to a satellite dish outside. They're watching a familiar film on HBO. Finally we sit on some sort of metal container and Brian begins to set up the camera.

In a few moments we start the interview. I have been warned that I will not get any provocative answers from FARC commanders like Ivan Rios. They are far too seasoned and savvy to let out a misdirected word. So we go through a well-choreographed dance. I lead with questions that must have been asked a million times before, and he answers with well-swathed declarations that proclaim nobility and the Marxist ideals that the guerrillas firmly believe. He dispenses the party lines smoothly. The FARC claims it is fighting a war on behalf of the campesinos—or poor farmers—whom they claim the government is not looking out for. They don't like the word *kidnapping* but admit that they are involved in "selective retentions" for specific reasons. They do indeed tax narco-traffickers on coca and poppy produced in the fields, but they are not at all involved in the production and/or trafficking of the drugs themselves. They are socially aware, he notes. They understand the decadence of drugs, especially on the young, and they are concerned. After about twenty minutes, he nods and signals that's it. We're done. He wins.

Brian begins to break down the camera.

"The killings," Rios says. "You have questions about the killings." His eyes are locked on mine once again.

"Yes," I manage to spit out.

"No camera."

"Okay."

"War is violent. And in war, there are casualties."

I interrupt him and suggest that most of the casualties in Colombia are innocent people, not warriors.

"My innocents die as well. Just because my soldiers are trained to kill, does that make them less innocent? They are children." He points to a group of young rebels in the clearing, playing volleyball where a court has been set up in the dirt. "They carry out their duty as warriors—they fight in a war that many of them don't understand."

This is similar to the situation of many of the farmers the FARC claims to be working for. They too do not really know what it is they are growing or, more specifically, what the raw coca and poppy they produce is eventually used for. For them, the crops are simply a means to an end, a product that enables their survival. So although they are complicit in the war around them, the guerrillas and the farmers, perhaps they are victims of forces larger than themselves. At the very least, it's a viable theory.

I mention to Commander Rios that I have traveled around the world in the past year, visiting one war-torn region after another. Many times I see similarities and analogies, but in Colombia something is distinct. Whereas in the rest of the world men kill one another over ideals, different versions of God, and under which God's name a land should exist, in Colombia it seems that people don't die for ideals. People die because of money. People die because there is a fight to control the huge financial rewards that come from the trafficking of cocaine and heroin. Something about this bothers me, because men driven by ideals, even when absurd, seem rather different from men driven to kill by the desire to line their pockets. A soul that kills for faith, though heinous, is not empty. A soul that kills for money, to me, seems devoid.

"When a man dies, does he care for the reason why?" Rios asks.

I don't know. I have not died.

Rios doesn't smile.

I am scared to ask my question: Doesn't he feel sickened by the killing of innocent people solely for money?

"War is ugly. And in war, there can be no morality. There can be no compassion. Because if it is not someone else who loses their life, then it is my boy—or my girl. Does this make me a bad man—an evil man?"

It's not a rhetorical question, because with the cameras off, Commander Rios is not a man of rhetoric.

I make no motion with my head, neither a nod nor a shake.

"In Colombia we have a shared experience we call a war. In the middle we have the drugs. And the drugs mean money, lots of money. We sell our services and protect the fields so that the narco-traffickers can have their business and so that the campesinos can have some sort of life."

Commander Rios doesn't mention it, but the paramilitaries are in the same line of work. They too are hired by narco-traffickers to protect the coca and poppy fields. Their methods are vicious, and they are a constant threat to anyone in Colombia.

"Without each other, we don't exist. It takes two to make the dance."

The expression, of course, is "It takes two to tango," but it gets lost in the translation. And in this case, there are more than two partners. Besides the FARC and the government, there is the paramilitary, the drug cartels, groups of *sicarios*—or teenage assassins hired by the cartels to carry out business—and several other, less heralded rebel groups. Their survival is dependent on the drug trade, and fortunately for them, the drug trade is as strong as ever.

"They may be our enemies," Rios says in reference to the FARC's combatants, "but they are also the only reason we exist, the only reason I sit here."

Life is a relationship. No matter how you look at it and from whatever scale, the rule applies. Commander Rios seems to understand this. His very existence is predicated on a vicious war, born from drug money. Take away the war, take away the FARC, and take away the commander. He is able to reference his soldiers, the jovial teenagers, and the poor farmers out in the fields and say that they are victims, but he knows that he cannot say that about himself, that he will not earn much sympathy. But is that true? Is it true that he, too, that warriors around the world, killers in gruesome wars, are helplessly playing out roles that all of us are complicit in?

That's right, all of *us.* For Commander Rios has failed to include one more element in the war in Colombia that he has outlined. The United States is the biggest customer of illegal drugs from Colombia. Eighty percent of the illegal drugs in the United States come from Colombia. If the money from the drugs is the blood that provides life for the war, then the United States is the foreign organ from where the money is hemorrhaging. When I mention this, Commander Rios nods, straight-faced.

"It would be impolite to place the blame."

His expression doesn't change, and I know once again that he means what he says.

"Maybe there will be a day that we can all offer forgiveness, just not now."

Day Six

The following day, flying back from San Vicente to Bogotá in a bumpy twin-engine Cessna, I think of my conversation with Commander Rios. I think about the idea of the war in Colombia as a huge web that has ensnared so many different players. Is war really a trap that sooner or later becomes inescapable?

And then it strikes me that Commander Rios had said something with some unexpected significance.

"You know, it was a great mistake what happened with the Americans last year." He was, of course, referring to the three Americans—the same ones that Amanda mentioned on my trip down to Colombia—who had been picked up in the jungle and summarily executed. I had seen it as a form statement, not worthy of much analysis. But now I wondered, why did he see this one act worthy of mention? Why did he consider this one act regrettable when kidnappings and murders at the hands of the FARC are daily occurrences in Colombia?

"There are few Americans down in this part of the country. People see them and are suspicious. It was a very bad mistake." He looked me in the eye again and repeated once more, "We're very sorry for the Americans." I felt awkward, as if offered an apology I didn't deserve or feel entitled to accept. But I wanted to nevertheless. And still I didn't—I didn't say anything at all.

He too would say no more, our conversation meandered away from this subtle, perhaps premeditated, slipup.

Had he asked me for forgiveness? Why had I wanted to offer it to him? I was reminded once more of my bus adventure in Pakistan, where out of nowhere a stranger had reached out and offered me simple human support and compassion in the face of chaos. It was not unlike the larger chaos in Colombia, where, in a war with so many complicit characters, it seemed for a brief moment that Commander Rios and I had shared a very human and compassionate moment. He *was* sorry. And I knew it. As our plane climbed higher above San Vicente and the dense jungles where many FARC camps hide out, where teenagers polish their guns in preparation for their next kill while watching HBO, I could not help thinking that maybe, maybe Commander Rios had shown me the first step as to how a war can be resolved.

Familiar Strangers

Now an old man, Buddha made one final pilgrimage to the small village that he knew would serve as his final resting place. A loyal servant who had followed him fell into a deep depression when he sensed his teacher would soon no longer be with him. "Don't go," he pleaded with Buddha. But he would go. "Don't worry," he calmed his student, holding his hand. "All things in this world are transient, including me—so don't be attached even to me." And like that, he smiled, closed his eyes, and softly allowed death to wash over him.

Death

"Let's talk about the meaning of life, shall we?" Papa cracks the white shell of a boiled egg and dusts some salt from between his fingers on the raw insides. An auxiliary supply of ten eggs rolls around beside him on his makeshift bed.

Many know him as some new-age guru or mystical mind that appears regularly on Larry King, but I know him as Dad—

more specifically Papa, as my sister, Mallika, and I have called him all our lives. But Papa, at times, is no less lofty in his conversations with us than he is in some of his biggest best-sellers.

The station outside starts to roll by, moving gently across my window. We're traveling the great Indian rail, the world's largest rail system and we're aboard one of the old Indian trains that travels from the Old Delhi station east to the holy cities all along the holy Ganges River. It's an all-night train, and families pack into rudimentary cabins that can be converted to sleeping cabins by lowering the benches that hang overhead. Technically, no more than four people can fit—one on each berth. But nevertheless you will see Indian families packing six, seven, conceivably even eight individuals in a single cabin. Those of us who are Americanized however—my parents included, since they have spent close to thirty years in the United States—struggle to find comfort on our own padded platform beds. We've crowded into three cabins—the four of my family in our cabin, family friends and a documentary film crew in the adjoining cabins.

The journey began in Delhi late in the evening. After a few hours we had stopped for twenty minutes in some lonely station. The station had been dark, lit only by the predawn glow and some dim, yellow fluorescent lights that hung overhead. Out on the platform, a few beggars had been slumped over on the ground, buried beneath thick burlap rags. It was cool out beneath the early morning mist that rolled through the station. A tea vendor outside had been walking beside the train cars, holding up a steaming kettle to some of the open windows where teacups held in outstretched arms reached out.

Papa and I had jumped out of the train when we felt it stop. We were hungry but discovered the only food available was bags of barbecue potato chips, the barely visible expiration date reading several years ago, and an old vendor who was willing to boil some eggs for us. Papa had walked across the platform to the empty track, where he and a few other men lined up, pissing into the basin.

I, therefore, had been left alone and charged with getting us some food. I nodded my head at the vendor, a motion that concealed my primitive Hindi. Papa returned and, looking on hungrily, suggested that we get at least a dozen eggs. We'd gather up some salt and *chaat masasla,* he said, and then be able to store the eggs for however many more hours we'd be on the train. Who knew when we'd next get a good, sanitized meal? Papa walked away, leaving me to explain this to the egg vendor.

I nodded again and ordered up *bara unda*—the extent of my Hindi. Ten minutes later the order was ready. Just then the train whistled sharply and I handed over a fistful of crumpled, colored rupees to the vendor. He nodded with a smile.

I asked him for a bag, but once again he just nodded and turned away, leaving the dozen boiled eggs teetering perilously on the chipped wooden countertop. Papa had already jumped onto the train and retreated to our cabin, where my sister and mother were still presumably asleep—leaving me alone to transport the dozen eggs. Seeing the train gently lurch its way forward, I did what I had to do, shoved the eggs against my chest inside of my jacket and dashed toward the train, jumping on as it gradually moved forward.

"You know, Gotham," Papa says back on the train as he peels away more of the shell of egg number one, "before we left Delhi, I heard that one of my classmates from medical school passed away. It was from heart disease, you know? Complications, cardiac arrest. He was very young, my age."

Papa's eyes are focused on his egg. "It's odd that only in

death somehow, do you start to think of and seek the meaning of life."

Papa, of course, seems to think about the meaning of life more than your average person. In short, he's built a career on it, sent his two kids through college on it, and built a very comfortable life for his family on it. But there remain moments—moments like these—that are beyond the fodder for the best-sellers.

"Karan"—He nods—"yes, that's it, Karan and I used to study together, smoke on our breaks together, go out for drinks afterward together." He smiles and then frowns very quickly. "You don't smoke, do you, Gotham?"

"No, Papa."

I get occasional checkups like this one. Papa knows his own lifestyle as a young student is not exactly a stellar model. He's never told me flat out not to drink and smoke but has been clear about his misgivings for having indulged so much in his youth. He knows I detest the idea of smoking, and he's come to bear the slight discomfort of my ordering unusual alcohols when we go out for dinner. About twenty years ago, when he first started meditating, he stopped cold turkey, cigarettes and booze, and never so much as looked at them again. I've always admired that.

But even Papa, who writes books and lectures endlessly about reversal of aging and timelessness, seems to have moments when he is brought up short by his mortality.

"Do you think about death, Papa?"

"Not really," he says, and smiles. "I think I am rather addicted to life."

He is still a very young man, and he lives with an enthusiasm and energy that would rival a teenager. The adventures we've been on all our lives are always rooted in his sense of curiosity about the world out there. It is remarkable to me how he maintains the energy to tackle a million tasks at once, to operate so efficiently on such little sleep.

"Are you afraid of death, Papa?"

"I hope not. Because only when you are prepared to die are you honestly prepared to live—I'm working on it."

We stopped because of a landfall. The road had literally been covered by the mountain.

In the foothills of the Himalayas of Kashmir, the rains sweep through with little warning at all. When they come, they come with a fury that is both bewildering and ecstatic. The rains fill up riverbeds that moments before were dry, rocky landfills. They cause waterfalls to cascade down from the hills and wash over the plains. And they cause landfalls, landfalls that invariably cause large chunks of the mountainside to lose their grip and fall into the roadway.

But in India, especially in the far reaches and outposts of the ancient country, this is not seen as much of a problem. An obstacle, perhaps, but a manageable obstacle that simply requires time, patience, and manpower to overcome—three elements that are not in short supply in India.

It is the second time in two days that a landslide has blocked our way. For some odd reason, despite or perhaps because of all the bureaucracy of the Indian government, Mitchell and I had been approved to head out with an army convoy in an effort to reach Kargil—the northernmost point of Kashmir, where some of the more intense fighting had been taking place in recent months between the Indian and Pakistani armies. The journey would require about an eight-hour drive—under good conditions.

Major Purshottam had arrived at our hotel in Sri Nagar promptly at ten A.M., insistent that we head out on time so that we travel with the army convoy in daylight. Of course, the roads in this part of the country are always implicitly unsafe—full of violence, terror, bloodshed, every step of the way—so to further ensure our safety, the army had ordered us to travel as part of their convoy: a long train of vehicles that would travel together, transporting men, equipment, and other supplies to the front lines in the north.

Again there would be no bathroom breaks, no stops for food or drink or for any other reason. But based on our experience the day before, having seen one of the army trucks flipped on its side by a remote explosive device that caused three casualties, none of us was in any mood for recreation anyway. In fact, things had turned rather somber. Now, as I scanned the local papers in the morning, counting the number of casualties racked up the day before, the war seemed far more real to me. No longer were they meaningless names or empty obituaries; they had become real people, young boys, victims of a world gone wrong.

Major Purshottam, of course, seemed hit hardest. Yet he was also the most used to it—the daily casualty count of "his boys," as he liked to call them. Like many soldiers, he had a strong sense of allegiance, pledging a loyalty to anyone who trusted him or his uniform for protection from the adversaries out in the hills. Might tomorrow be the day that his name or even ours would show up in the morning newspaper, listed as a casualty of war? Only then might a life be transformed into some lesson learned from death.

For now the major was just a middle-aged soldier—someone in whose hands we had casually invested our well-being. We chatted off and on, passing the time, until four hours into the trip I fell asleep in the rear of the van.

When I awoke, we had done what we weren't supposed to: we had stopped in the middle of the road—wedged ourselves in the shadows of mountains on all sides of us.

Soon a dispatch from the front of the convoy relayed the situation. A landslide brought on by the heavy rains had washed the mountainside straight into the roadway. But it was only three o'clock in the afternoon, there was still plenty of sunlight guarding us from the threat of the rebels.

"Not to worry." Major Purshottam waved his hand from the front seat as if pushing away some wall of anxiety that separated us from him. "We have plenty of time to get there."

So I settled back again, squeezing myself in between some of our boxy equipment, determined not to let any fear well up inside of me.

"I wonder if you might have seen—I think it was several weeks ago—an article in *India Today*." Major Purshottam looked back from the front.

I nodded my head gingerly, just enough to feign some sort of familiarity.

"The article was written by one of our boys here in Kargil—in fact, it was a letter from one of the boys to his new wife back in one of the villages." The major turned fully now and settled into a more comfortable posture as the driver shut off the engine of the van—a sure sign we weren't to be moving for some time.

"It was a beautiful letter, in fact, all about the Gita."

The Gita, of course, is a short piece of scripture that Hindus revere in much the same ways that Christians do the Bible, Muslims the Koran, or Jews the Torah. The Gita is a small discourse that is part of a much larger epic—the Mahabharata—which literally translates as the "epic story of India." The story of the Mahabharata is about two sets of rival cousins pitted against one another their entire lives, a feud that culminates in their confronting each other on the great battle plains of Kurukshetra, the arid desert plains not far from modern-day Delhi.

The event the Gita portrays can be only a few minutes long, sixty at most, dropped in the middle of the gigantic epic. The story revolves around a solitary conversation between Lord Krishna and the great warrior Arjuna. As the war is just about to get under way, the huge armies facing each other, awaiting the sound of the conch shell to signal the beginning of the fight, Arjuna urges his charioteer, Lord Krishna, to trot out in the middle of the field so he can get one last, close look at his adversaries before the battle begins.

Lord Krishna complies, and when they reach the center of the battlefield, Arjuna loses his grip on his favorite weapon—his bow and arrow—and, even worse, loses his poise. Looking closely at the faces of his adversaries—his own cousins, uncles, nephews, teachers, and students he has grown up with—he falls back, convinced that the war he is about to fight is wrong.

"No," he tells Krishna, "I will not fight. I will not draw the blood of my own kin for this. I surrender."

Herein begins the heart of the Gita. Krishna responds by talking to Arjuna about the dharma of every man—the duty he has to play out his role for his station in life. While he professes to understand Arjuna's confusion, he champions the importance of the larger sense of obligation, the importance of fighting the fight even amid the confusion. He also convinces Arjun that *real surrender* is the ability to fight, to take part in the action of the world, but to remain detached from the outcome.

"In the letter from the soldier," Major Purshottam continues, "he told his wife how much he missed her. About how much he missed their newborn baby girl. He also talks about the war, about the difficulty in killing when the ideas for which you're fighting aren't so clear."

The major fixed his eyes on Mitch and then me. "You know, Mitchell, Gotham, we try our very hardest to train the boys and explain the war to them, but they don't always understand."

I was sure at the time that this throwaway disclaimer would have some timely significance, but at the present moment I wasn't sure what it was. So I dismissed it with another rhythmic nod of the head.

"But in the letter, he talked about the warrior's dharma—that the warrior's purpose is to fight, not to go against the way of the world, but to play out his role willingly within it." He paused. "It really was quite beautiful."

But something alarmed me—the same thing that has always alarmed me about the Gita, which is that like most other pieces of scripture, presumably it's not to be taken literally all the time. In other words, it'd be nice to think that not all conflicts require war and the duty of the warrior for resolution. I mentioned this to the major, who shook his head vigorously.

"The path of life often leads down unfamiliar roads. It's not always clear why you are where you are or how you got there. The important thing is to fulfill your duty once you are there. And that requires a certain fearlessness—an ability to detach and be free."

But war in the modern day seems to have more to do with nationalism and patriotism, slogans and strategies, oil and economy, than the passions of warriors.

"Yes, but soldiers must do the fighting, not the politicians.

And so it is in the soldier that you find the real reasons that they are able to fight.

"In this case, with the soldier, he understood it. He knew himself that he wasn't sure why there was a war, why he was fighting it. But he had found freedom. He had surrendered, and that is the way the warrior finds final triumph."

A silence ensued. Up ahead, a few young soldiers smoked cigarettes, showing no signs of fear being stuck out in the middle of nowhere. I myself knew I had been suckered by them, by Major Purshottam, into believing that there was some romance in their warring. It's the type of sentimentality that makes war movies and sells novels, or in this case *India Today* issues.

I asked the question, though I already knew the answer.

Did the soldier die?

"I'm quite sure that he did."

About an hour later we had moved on in our conversation. As the sky started to settle into dusk, it no longer seemed appropriate to sit around and talk about the dangers lurking on the roads. In fact, now it was as if we were purposely avoiding it. Our only movement in the past few hours had been backward. About half an hour earlier, Major Purshottam had instructed our driver to back our van away from one of the army trucks. He made no direct mention why, but it was clear once again that the threat of the convoy being attacked was beginning to encroach on us. Now out of the shadows of the big army trucks, we started to talk about family.

During a lull in the conversation, Mitch mentioned my father's name. Major Purshottam tilted his head and then shook it, saying it didn't ring a bell to him.

"There is, however, another doctor in Delhi by the same name—far older, but very famous himself."

When he mentioned that the famous Dr. Chopra was a cardiologist and lived in a suburb of Delhi called Defense Colony, it clicked. Indeed, it was not my father, it was my grandfather the major was familiar with. And, as it turns out, Major Purshottam's mother had passed through my grandparents' home in New Delhi during a pilgrimage the year before. She had been accompanying her lifelong friend and Major Purshottam's godmother—Ama—who had been widowed at an early age with a young daughter and had been befriended by my grandparents more than half a century ago. The young daughter—Shoba—had grown up like a sister to my father and when I was born had become my godmother.

"In a nation of one billion people, what are the chances?" Major Purshottam smiled. "What are the chances that my godmother would be the mother of yours and that here we would be sitting trapped by a mountain in the road? The world, Gotham, is full it seems of familiar strangers."

Soon dusk turned to dark. Though the stars shone like diamonds stuck to black velvet, the threat of impending terror cast a shadow on the scene. Though the road was beginning to clear, it was determined that vehicles carrying nonmilitary personnel should head for the capital. That meant us. Within minutes we were heading back beneath the night sky to Srinagar.

Once again we had joined up with a caravan of other cars and vans, blazing in a trail of exhaust through the night. The roads were especially dark because there were no lights—no streetlights, just the brief intermittent flickers of some of the vehicles' headlights as they raced along the road. Once again for safety reasons, so that the vehicles were not easily detected, we had been instructed not to use our lights and to stay at a steady clip on the road, and for the passengers to stay away from the windows.

The drive itself lasted another six and a half hours and by the time we reached the base camp, the sun was beginning to dance above the foothills.

Once more, we moved to Major Purshottam's small office.

"I would die for a cup of *chai*." He smiled at us and began his preparations. This, we had now learned, was one of his favorite lines.

As he poured the hot water in three small china cups, he spoke. "Another day death is cheated."

I had not thought of it in such dramatic terms, but now that it was over, I was willing to romanticize it.

"When death comes, be certain that you are prepared for it. For being prepared to die is the only way to live." Major Purshottam stirred the tea leaves, letting them saturate in the boiling water.

"Are you prepared for death?" Mitch inquired as he took a cup of *chai* from the major.

The major smiled as he took the first sip of the *chai* he so loved.

"I believe I am."

An hour later, Mitch and I picked up our gear, said our good-byes, climbed aboard our jeep, and headed back for the hotel. The following day we boarded our plane and headed back for Delhi. Within a week I was back in Los Angeles, sitting in an edit facility, trying to cut out sound bites that would capture moments from our trip. The words and conversations with Major Purshottam lingered, even though the esoteric questions of the meaning of his life, his boys' lives, my own, all of ours, didn't seem so immediate in the comfort of my metropolitan existence. In the ensuing months, I gathered more stories in

Colombia, Russia, and Sri Lanka that would raise still more probing questions. I also carried on with my life, developing projects, making contacts and contracts, attending parties, doing the things that twentysomethings do.

And then one day, nearly four months after sitting in Major Purshottam's office, while scanning the *New York Times,* I discovered a small sidebar that mentioned an Indian army officer— R. K. Purshottam—killed in the line of duty while protecting two journalists in his office from an attack of "armed militants" who had descended from the hills.

Even his teacup was shattered, the newspaper reported.

In the Indian city of Varanasi, death is a way of life. Many men from traditional Hindu families all over India finalize their lives by retiring to these crowded village streets along the holy Ganges River. But retirement in Varanasi is unlike anywhere else in the world. The old men in the streets wander seemingly aimlessly, without the concerns of return dividends on 401(k) plans, Social Security benefits, and subsidized Medicaid plans. They dally in silence, sit by the sides of the streets, sip hot tea at crumbling stalls, waiting—waiting for death to come and escort them to the next world.

Most of these elderly men believe in the Vedantic tradition that breaks life up into four sections. The first twenty-five years are to be spent "learning," the next twenty-five "earning" and raising a family, the third twenty-five giving charity, and the final twenty-five—or however long it lasts—in meditation, gradually surrendering all of one's possessions, preparing for death. In that tradition, the city of Varanasi has become the hub for these men in the final stages of their lives. Having left their families safe and secure, they are here passing the time until the final moment, the final mystery that relieves them of their duty to life.

When at last these older men are taken by death, another ritual occurs in Varanasi, the ritual for which the ancient city is most famous for—cremations. Ghats line the edges of the Ganges River, and every day and night countless cremations take place. It's hard to spell out exactly the procedure for these cremations, because as with everything else in India, there doesn't seem to be any standard routine. As for my own knowledge of how death is handled in Varanasi, all I can explain is what I saw one night with my father.

It was Christmas Eve when we arrived in Varanasi. The train was running a standard six hours late, and by the time we trudged into our hotel darkness had descended on the town. Only the lobby seemed to be making an effort to conjure up some holiday spirit. Loose green and red ribbons hung over the reception counter. A browned-out wreath was tacked to the splintered wall. And in cursive writing across a chalkboard behind the counter just below the room rates ($51 per double) ran the words *Happy Christmas.*

"Merry Christmas," one of our travel companions said, smiling at the receptionist as she began to check in.

"Happy Christmas," she replied.

A few minutes later we were all assigned our rooms. A young man named Shiv who was traveling with us caught up to our group as we waited for the elevator to take us up to our rooms. *"Deepak, sahib,"* he addressed my father, looking at me.

"Should you want to go to the ghats and do the filming, perhaps this is the best night."

We had spent nearly ten hours traveling to Varanasi, and all of us were worn out. Ryan, the field producer for the doc film crew that was accompanying us as part of one of my dad's latest projects, seemed panicked at the thought of going out again. But after Shiv declared that this would really be our only opportunity to go out to the cremation grounds, Ryan knew that the opportunity must be seized. We all agreed to reassemble in the lobby in a few minutes and head out to the cremation grounds.

Within half an hour, eight of us—all men, as we had been instructed by Shiv that only men were allowed—jammed in two rickety Ambassador cars and headed for the center of the city. At ten-thirty the streets were empty, spotted by just a few lonely cows snorting through heaps of trash collected by the side of the road.

A few minutes later, we arrived at an empty lot. Our driver rolled the car to a stop and jumped out. This, I supposed, was our signal that we had arrived. We all spilled from the cars and collected outside. Shiv told us to wait for him and then crossed the street and slipped into one of the narrow alleyways.

"Gotham," my father called me over beside him, "stay with me."

Those were the only words we'd speak for the next thirty minutes, for a moment later Shiv returned and instructed us to follow him quietly.

We had picked up a few assorted hangers-on, young men who wanted to translate, guide, and explain to us what we would soon see.

But as we began our march across the street and into the aforementioned alleyway, they too fell away, leaving us to head into a maze of still more narrow alleyways that would lead us where we wanted to go.

Right, then left, then left again, a sharp right, and twenty steps later another sharp right. I was lost within ten minutes, but Shiv seemed to know his way, aggressively shooting down the slippery paths as we all struggled to keep up with him.

An eerie quiet reigned. Curious merchants spied out from their open storefronts. Two older men we passed sat silently on a crumbling step, sharing a thin *bidi* cigarette. We came and went before their eyes—and none of them even blinked at the oddity of so many foreigners dashing through their lives with camera equipment on Christmas Eve.

Every once in a while, we'd have to dance out of the way, squeeze up against the wall, and nudge by a trash-grazing cow, a skinny goat, or hungry dog. But no one said anything. All of us, it seemed, knew we were headed to see something unique—the ghats at the banks of the Ganges River, the shores of death.

"Do you remember, Gotham, when you were very young meeting your great-grandfather?" Papa asks while peeling away the shell of boiled egg number two. He's crouched back on his bottom bunk, his face half-covered by the shadow cast from the bunk hanging overhead.

I do. We called him Bouji. And though I was very young when we met, vague memories still swim around my head. They're not so much visual memories of events as much as they are blurred images, smells, sounds, all packaged into mismatched moments that are difficult to string together. I remember being four years old and Bouji being almost one hundred. I remember sitting on his lap and looking at the many folds in his face. I remember his smell—he smelled old. I remember the house, that decrepit house on Babar Road that has been in my family's possession for generations, in which living room my father was actually born. I remember the noise. There was always a lot of noise because there was lots of family, four generations' worth screaming and yelling, competing for attention. And I remember Bouji's eyes, deep and brown like mine, windows to some century that for the most part existed before I did.

"Bouji died happy. Very few people die happy, satisfied with the life they've lived, prepared to move on."

Bouji, of course, was nearly one hundred years old when he passed. He had plenty to be happy about, having lived to see four generations of his family grow and mature. But now it's not clear to me whether my dad is happy, ready. Personally I hate to think about it, the death of my parents. I can safely say that I am not ready for it. But today, early this winter morning on this train headed for holy cities that celebrate death, Papa wants to talk about death. And I oblige him.

"You know, Gotham, in the hospital you get pretty used to death. And with most deaths, you see the same stages when someone realizes they most likely won't make it—panic, fear, resistance, denial, resignation. You can mix in some others, anger, denial—peace—but not often. Most people don't ponder their own death before they meet it, so when it knocks on their door, they peer through the peephole and are terrified by what they see."

To be honest, I probably belong in that camp as well. Despite how often I venture to violent places, I suspend thinking of death for fear of my absolute ignorance of what it means. And over and above that, it strikes me as depressing to think about death in the midst of living.

"True." Papa nods. "But that's because no one ever taught us how to die, and most of us equate death with suffering. And that's not the hard-and-fast case. Maybe death shouldn't be depressing. Maybe in death there should be as much of a celebration as there is in birth. After all, birth and death are part of the same revolving door—one way in, the other out, coming and going to and from the same endless eternity."

It all makes some sort of poetic sense, and as long as we are talking about death, I want direct advice from Papa on how to deal with it. Perhaps he has some profound message of how to accept and understand death. If so, I want it.

"It's not that difficult. Appreciate life. If today were your last day, would everyone you love know that you love them? And admire death the same way. Perhaps there is no understanding death, because who knows what's on the other side? But watch closely when you get a chance and admire it."

I imagine if ever there was a place that resembles Dante's Inferno, then the ghats of Varanasi are it. Beneath the midnight sky, towering fires reach supreme heights. Thick black smoke plumes upward before merging into the darkness of the sky. An army of charnel men carry out their duties, marching to and fro, handling bodies, shifting them from here to there as if they are farmers charged with gathering grain at harvest. Lean, hungry dogs wander lethargically through the mud coagulated in mounds beside corpses lain out side by side. Cows and goats meander aimlessly as well, snorting listlessly in search of a crumb to eat. The water's edge is still, absent of any ebb and flow, thick like a muddy marsh, stolen of any life itself. The shores of death in Varanasi are an ugly place, but they are beautiful as well.

The caretakers of these places are "untouchable" young men charged with the burden of transporting cadavers and their souls from this world to the next.

It's not an easy job, and it doesn't come with much respect.

Among the five castes in India—though it is a dying system—harijans, or "untouchables," are still considered the lowest of the low. Ironically, though, it is these men who are responsible for one of the most precious journeys that a loved one will venture on—the journey to rest in peace.

The ghats by the river's edge in Varanasi are their office. And when you arrive at their office, the first images can be rather shocking. Individually wrapped bodies lined up side by side, waiting for their turn. When their turn does arrive, they are hoisted by a charnel onto a smoking heap of sticks and other flammable items. The charnel delicately tucks in their arms, straightens their legs, ensures that all their skin is covered, and then ignites the pyre. If the flames wane, he'll shuffle around some sticks, fan the flames, and make sure the job is done right. There are many details to attend to, a random assortment of tiny tasks required so that the ritual is done right and death can be fully achieved. One detail that stands out occurs when the charnel takes a small welded hammer and smashes it onto the skull of the deceased. What appears as a gruesome act of profanity is actually a motion of facility that enables the face and brain to burn more efficiently and ease the transition of the physical body into something more immaterial. Traditionalists insist that if this seemingly violent act is not performed correctly, the soul will not properly be released from the body.

When the charnel is finished, he'll gather the ashes, place them in a vat, and stick it in one of the splintered boats docked at the water's edge. When the boat is full, he'll paddle it out to the middle of the river, far enough from the bathers who will wash in the same river come dawn, and spill out the ashes until they swirl beneath the surface of the water. He does his routine mechanically but with a subtle devotion that belies his outright efficiency. He practices his job like you or me, only his job is anything but routine, for he is the usher of death itself.

Many families in India observe the traditional death rituals. The body is wrapped in white cloth not unlike an Egyptian mummy. Gold threads are laced with smooth silks and then meshed with traditional orange garlands. This is how one is dressed, prepared for the final journey toward eternity. But after tears are shed, good-byes uttered, and prayers recited by assigned holy men, the body itself is handed over to the charnel man—the anonymous bearer entrusted to escort the soul to its final resting place. They have no emotional attachment to these souls, but they do have a sworn duty. They are like bus drivers determined to deliver their passengers to the right destination while observing the speed limit.

Looking on at their work, Death reveals another face. A young boy—one of the charnel's sons who himself one day will most likely be a cremator—tiptoes among some of the bodies, playfully jabbing some of the corpses and then shooing away an idle goat sniffing at the thigh of one. The stench of death is strong, ash burning the nostrils, compelling the eyes to water. But there is a rhythm to their work. The charnels are diligent, obliquely compassionate, but, above all else, efficient. Here death is not scary or obtrusive, it is merely routine.

The sun has risen now and blazes a heat along the vast plains that warms the cabins of the train. At the ends of the train cars are the entryways—large enough spaces for a few people to share a smoke, engage in a conversation, or simply watch the scenery rush by outside. The doorways have been opened to the outside so the wind gusts in. Papa and I move to the entryway to get away from the eggs and out of the claustrophobic cabin. There are two old men squatting side by side. Their faces are worn, rugged, so aged that they are indeed charming. Between them is an ornamented pipe—a large Persian-style bong that filters flavored tobacco and then shoots it through a velvet tube to its smoker. The men pass it from one to another, casually taking deep, pleasurable hits, a glassy glaze washing over their eyes.

We exchange nods with them, and they remark something to Papa in Punjabi.

Papa replies with a smile and puts his hand on my shoulder. The two men nod, smiling at me.

Papa asks them where they are going, and one of the men responds in a thick accent.

"Varanasi."

What for?

"*Sanyas,*" the other man says, blowing out a lungful of lemon-scented smoke. *Sanyas* is the term that refers to silence—what old men undertake when they retire to the city of Varanasi.

So these are indeed the men, live and in person, the ones headed for the city of death, ready to wait for their reservation with the end. They hardly look scared or anxious. In fact, I cannot imagine a more serene set.

In our conversation on death, Papa has used words like "freedom," "detachment," "surrender," and looking at these two men, I understand the terminology truly for the first time. They have indeed surrendered for the final time, given away their fear of the unknown, and are now free to coast through the remainder of their lives without the anxious expectation of what lurks on the other side of tomorrow.

They look happy, at ease, prepared for the final adventure.

Papa and I stare at them. That's how we'd like to be. We're working on it. We'll get there.

The world outside the window is rushing by. We're moving quickly now, shooting through the plains, intermittently rushing through crowded villages with countless faces that blur on by. Each place is home to a million stories—maybe more—most of which we'll never know.

Both of us stare at the plains outside, the strange but familiar world.

"At the end it'll have been a very interesting trip," Papa says, his eyes fixed outside on the yellow haze hovering over the dusty earth.

"What, Varanasi?"

"All of it, baby," he says tenderly, "all of it."

Acknowledgments

I would like to express my thanks and gratitude to all of the following people who made this book possible:

My family: Your love, support, trust, and tolerance to allow me to go out adventure after adventure is the source for every story.

Candice: what can I say . . . all of the above and more. I have a feeling we have a few more adventures upon us. I love you.

My Editor Trace Murphy: whose guidance, patience, and touch has made all of this possible and special.

My Producers: To everyone at Channel One who have been the facilitators in many adventures and encounters at the edge of reality. Special thanks to Mitch, Chris, Laura, Auzzie, Jim, Morgan, Brian, Andy, Scott—your courage, companionship, and cool has made it all a lot of fun.